Raton

History

Mystery

and

More

Raton
History
Mystery
and
More

by

Mike J. Pappas

Raton
History Mystery and More

by

Mike J. Pappas

Cover Art by Jim Mullings

Published by Coda Publications
P.O.B.71, Raton, New Mexico 87740

Printed in the United States of America

ISBN 0-910390-69-X
Library of Congress Control Number
L.C. 2003109178

Table of Contents

Bird's eye view of Raton in 1882

Raton History Mystery and More

Introduction

I became involved with the history of Raton when I wrote a series of articles for *The Raton Range*, called *A Flea in the Ear*. It is is an old expression that is defined as a word of advice, or in modern terminology, one's two cent's worth. *A Flea in the Ear* was basically an opinion, or editorial column, that reflected my personal opinions on everything from the weather to local politics.

One morning, over a cup of coffee with friends, one of Raton's old-timers told me the story of La Josie, Raton's infamous peg-legged lady-of-the-night. This story had never been published, so I decided to use it in my *Flea in the Ear* series. It was an instant success. Soon people were calling me to write more about the history of real life events that involved people and families that resided in Raton and the surrounding communities. It was not long before I acquired a wealth of historical data about Raton and the surrounding area.

Raton's history is well recorded in several books that include Father Stanley's *Raton Chronicle* and Jay Conway's *A Brief Community History of Raton*. Several "white" papers have been written about Raton, for example, Evlyn Shuler's *How Raton Began* and Kenneth Fordyce's *Willow Springs Ranch*. In addition, *The Official Souvenir of the State of New Mexico* from the Panama-California Exposition held in San Diego in 1915 reveals much about the early history of Raton. All of these documents are available at either the Arthur Johnson Memorial Library or the Raton Museum.

Typically, history is often recorded in a series of chronological events. For example, some of the events during Raton's early years might include the following:

- 1880 - The site for the Town of Raton was selected and the Santa Fe Railroad moved its offices from Otero, a boxcar community located about five miles south of Raton.
- 1881 - The Santa Fe Railroad completed construction of its roundhouse and machine shops.
- 1883 - The first public school opened in the Methodist Church.
- 1891 - A town government was organized.
- 1897 - The town was organized under a City Charter.
- 1899 - The county seat was moved from Springer to Raton.
- 1902 - A sanitary sewer system was installed.
- 1910 - The city created and built a municipal water works.
- 1912 - The Raton Public Library was built at Ripley Park.
- 1914 - The city erected a municipal building
- 1919 - Raton acquired the electric plant.

- 1920 - The City of Raton began paving streets.
- 1927 - Raton's first municipal swimming pool opened.
- 1928 - Goat Hill opened as a park.

As Raton grew, housing became a problem. Many new settlers had to live in tents while waiting for homes to be built. In the early 1900s these tents were located on an empty lot that now houses the El Portal Hotel building at Park Avenue and 3rd Street.

While this type of historical information is important and necessary, it does not always reveal many of the other wonderful, and some not so wonderful, events that transpired over the years. This book, therefore, is not a chronological history of Raton but rather a series of short stories about events of interest in Raton and the surrounding area that includes Colfax County and Southern Colorado. Some of the stories are light-hearted and fun. Others are informative, and some are sad, such as the mine disasters in Dawson.

Most of the information in this book was researched and should be relatively accurate. However, many of the stories were written from personal interviews with friends and citizens of the Raton area. The accuracy of these interviews may be subject to dispute. Several stories include my own personal observations and comments. My intent is not to distort history, but to give readers an insight into the many activities that occurred in our area over the years.

I hope you enjoy reading this series of short stories as much as I have enjoyed writing them.

Mike J. Pappas

Everyone loved a parade, such as this early 1890's event which is marching down First Street, then known as Railroad Avenue.

Raton Trivia

When I was researching the history of Raton I frequently found bits and pieces of history that were unusually interesting. Here are a few of them.

Apple Orchards

Colfax County was once a large apple-producing county. There were apple orchards from Cimarron to Miami. In 1893, M.M. Chase won a gold medal at the Chicago World's Fair with apples grown on the old Kit Carson Ranch near Cimarron.

The 1915 Official Souvenir of the State of New Mexico from the Panama-California Exposition at San Diego stated that in thirty-five years one large orchard has never produced a wormy apple out of thousands of bushels grown. The Urraca Ranch in Cimarron claimed it had 23,000 trees in its orchard and boasted that it never had a crop failure. The unanswered question is what happened to the apple industry? Why did it die out?

I visited with many old-timers from Cimarron and the surrounding area and no one really knows why. Many believe a long drought caused the trees to die. Others believe insect infestation killed the trees.

The Road to Trinidad, known as "Old Raton Pass".

Raton Pass of today is well known to many travelers. The old Raton Pass goes up Moulton to Goat Hill and beyond. You can still navigate some of the wicked hairpin curves going to the top for about a mile or so before it is closed to the public. The old pass, with all its hairpin curves, was very dangerous. A new highway to Trinidad was built around 1915 by the State of New Mexico using convict labor. Today, that highway is a part of U.S. Interstate 25. This picture, a postcard published around 1928, is from our Raton Museum.

A long walk to get the mail

Before 1878, the only place for Raton citizens to pick up mail was at the Clifton House, pictured above. It was located about six miles south of Raton. Stages brought the mail and left it there. The Clifton House was a hub of activity for both Raton citizens and travelers. Indians on their way to Cimarron for supplies often stopped here to rest. The first "Raton" Post Office authorization, granted in 1878, was designated as the Willow Springs Post Office.

If Otero had water, there would be no Raton

Otero, located about five miles south of Raton, was actually the end of track laid for the Atchison, Topeka and Santa Fe Railroad. It was a town for about twelve months. The town had a newspaper called the *Otero Optic* that printed its first story on May 22, 1879.

Lack of sufficient water forced the moving of Otero north to what is now Raton. Town buildings in Otero were literally put on railroad flatcars and transferred to Raton. Today, nothing is left of Otero. Many issues of the *Optic* newspaper can be found in archives of the Colfax County Clerks office in Raton.

Some elections were simple: Vote For, or Against

The Maxwell Land Grant was not popular among many Raton citizens. The late Evlyn Shuler, Raton's long-time librarian and historian, once wrote, "There was a great deal of bad feelings because a number of people came and settled on part of the Grant and felt, because they had settled there, that it was theirs. I can remember when the tickets for election were "Grant" and "Anti-Grant.""

You could tell Raton was a railroad town by its street names

Many of the streets of Raton had railroad names. For example, Tunnel Avenue (Fifth Street); Atchison Avenue (Fourth Street); Topeka Avenue (Third Street); Santa Fe Avenue (Second Street); and Railroad Avenue (First Street). I never did learn when and why the names were changed.

It paid to be the first-born

The first baby born in Raton arrived in a house on the western outskirts north of Climax Canyon. The Townsite Company gave the young lady a deed to the house and lot in which she was born.

Telephone service

The first telephone in Raton was installed in Dr. Shuler's home. It connected him with his office in the coal-mining town of Blossburg, located about five miles northwest of Raton, and several ranches. Another early telephone line from Raton was a private system built in 1891 between the Schroeder Drug Store on First Street and the Delno & Dwyer Ranch, 12 miles southeast of Raton.

Early birds

From Jay Conway's History of Raton - "One of the first permanent residents, Mr. John Jelfs, has been quoted in printed history as saying that, when he landed here in July, 1880, three inhabitants had already pitched their tents before him."

Gold fillings did not go to waste

Morticians in the 1800's and early 1900's had a common trademark. They all had gold nugget chains and watch fobs carried discreetly because the gold nuggets came from, you guessed it, the deceased's gold teeth. The gold nuggets were crudely made and one could tell they had been re-melted by an amateur. I did not believe this story until I actually saw one of the watch fobs.

Raton was not always the County Seat

The first county seat in Colfax County was in Elizabethtown. When Elizabethtown dwindled, the county seat was moved to Cimarron. Later it was relocated to Springer and later to Raton. There were a lot of hard feelings, political maneuverings and county feuding when Raton became the county seat. This, the original Court House built in Raton, was a magnificent brick structure. It housed the county jail and was the site of one of the hangings that you will read about in the story of Gus Mentzer.

Sources of Raton Trivia

For those of you who would like more detail on some of Raton's history, read Father Stanley's *Raton Chronicle*, Jay Conway's *A Brief Community History of Raton, NM*, Evlyn Shuler's *How Raton Began*, Kenneth Fordyce's *Willow Springs Ranch*, and *The official Souvenir of the State of New Mexico at the Panama-California Exposition, San Diego 1915*. All are on file at the Raton Public Library and the Raton Museum.

Want to stand on the orginal Santa Fe Trail? Ripley Park, in the north part of Raton, is located on the original Santa Fe Trail. The city's first library was built in Ripley Park with money from the Andrew Carnegie Foundation. Their grant totaled $12,000, plus $3000 in matching City funds to pay for the library's construction.

The first Santa Fe depot for Raton was built in the 1880's. .

A more modern depot was constructed in later years, then modified into the present structure that is the second most-used depot in the State of New Mexico.

George Honeyfield, in 1914, provided mail, freight and passenger service for Raton, Blossburg, Gardner, Swastika and Brilliamt.

From the cuspidor and brass foot-rail, to a lack of tables or chairs, Raton bars were for drinking and male-to-male socializing.

Raton's Red Light District

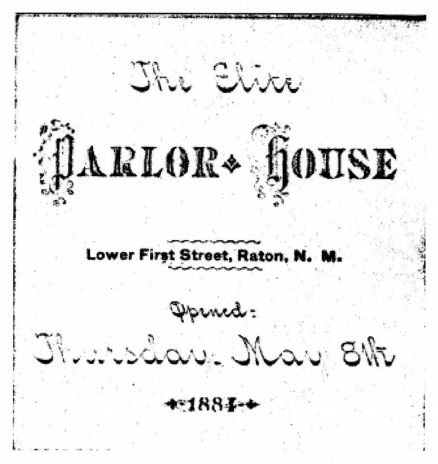

The inside message of this "Opening Day" invitation suggested that the recipient "Bring A Friend."

Everyone who is a history buff knows that "Red Light Districts" were abundant in the old West. Raton was no exception. In fact, it was an extremely lucrative business for many prostitutes because the county had hundreds of immigrant coal miners who had left their families in Europe to seek their fortunes in the land of Golden Opportunity. There was also an extremely large labor pool of railroad workers who manned the trains that shipped coal as far away as Mexico. And, of course, there was a scarcity of women for men to court. Accordingly, any attempt to explain the liberal policy of city government regarding prostitution would be an exercise in futility.

Red light district fattened city coffers

Raton's red-light district was very active in the late 1880's and early 1900's. While prostitution was not desired, the community, to "protect the fairer sex," tolerated it. Income to the city wasn't bad either. The monthly fine for prostitution was $8.50. In February 1908, 32 women paid a total of $272 in fines into the city coffers.

The red light district, which included several homes and businesses on First Street, was left alone as long as the ladies paid their fines on a regular basis. Then disaster struck. The city fathers discovered that the deputy who collected the fines only turned in $187.50 from the $272 assessed. The prostitutes were upset when they learned that their hard-earned money was being embezzled. The deputy was tried in court, and with testimony offered by the women, was found guilty and sentenced.

However, after they had voluntarily testified against the deputy, the women were fined $25 plus court costs! This angered the prostitutes because they had already paid their $8.50 monthly fine. A series of confrontations between the city fathers and the prostitutes followed. The women did not want to lose their livelihood and the City did not want to lose its income. As a compromise, the City Council voted to close all houses nearer than 700 feet from a church or hall. Things finally settled down and prostitution continued for the next few decades with the blessing of City Hall.

La Josie

One of my favorite stories about Raton's Red Light District is the story of a lady called La Josie whose real name is still unknown. La Josie was one of the most popular working ladies on Garcia Street's red-light district, located on Raton's East Side.

The story goes that La Josie had an accident in her youth and one of her legs had to be amputated. Like many amputees in those days, La Josie was fitted with a peg leg. She became so proficient using the peg leg that most people were unaware that she was handicapped except when she used her crutch on occasion.

La Josie was popular, not because of her charms, but because of her dancing ability. The story goes that after a couple of margaritas, and when the music became loud and fast, her dance partners could twirl her and she would spin on her peg leg like a top. Another version of her dancing ability was that she also used her crutch when dancing. Between the peg leg and the crutch, she would dance up a storm, spinning on either crutch or peg leg to measures of the same music..

La Josie had a friend and partner. Her name was *La Suave* - which, in Spanish, is pronounced "La-swha-vah." It means "The best." It was never known if La Josie's friend was the best in her profession or best as a dancer. Unfortunately, there is no written record of *La Suave*'s history and the "old timer" who told me the story of La Josie was not familiar with *La Suave*.

Another of my favorite stories about prostitution in Raton involves the worst fire in Raton's history which occurred in 1888 in a house of prostitution. (This was 20 years before the first official fire department for the City of Raton was organized in 1908.) It appears that one of the women threw a lighted lamp at a "gentleman" guest during an argument and nearly burned down the main business block.

At the time many local residents considered it a blessing since, according to the *Raton Reporter*, "It eradicated a notorious den of ill-fame and wiped out the existence of a lot of rat-trap houses which were a disgrace to First Street and to the City of Raton." The fire, to the disappointment of many Raton citizens did not eliminate the problem of prostitution. By the early 1900's, First Street had come back to life.!

Raton History Mystery and More

The Search for Oil

Raton's oil fever began in 1902 when an eminent geologist from Colorado, named Arthur Lakes, made a thorough examination of the area east and northeast of Raton. He found that the land in these areas "Abounds in surface indications of oil. " The report said the lands near Raton included:

· "A considerable thickness of shale carrying marine fossil and shells and other marine organisms that are supposed to be favorable to oil and in which, according to some geologist, the oil originates.

· "The probability of the occurrence of porous sandstone or sandy layers at uncertain intervals packed between these layers of shale, forming convenient storage reservoirs for oil or oil sands.

· "The structural position of the strata that it is on the slope of a gentle anticline, the anticlinal or broad arch structure being in high repute amongst oil men for oil occurrence."

There were other factors that motivated the search for oil. Among them was that Lakes reported signs of gas indicatiing that oil could be underground Rumor also had it that a man digging a hole for a well on the McCowen ranch ignited the gas in the well and was severely burned.

On June 26, 1902, a Colorado newspaper, *The Citizen,* reported:

"C.C. Hall has returned from Raton and brought with him rich specimens of oil-bearing rock and petrifications from the Raton oil fields. These specimens show that there is at Raton an extensive oil field, when developed, will make that city the center of a great oil industry. Mr. Hall will place the specimens on exhibition in the Commercial Club in this city.

"The company operating the Raton oil fields have $15,000 in cash in the bank with which to begin active work. A contract has been let to bore a well to a depth of 3,000 feet if necessary. The machinery of the boring company is now on the ground and work will begin on July 4.

"Colorado capitalalist are interested, with the people of Raton, in the company that will develop this promising oil field and the chances are good that within a few weeks *The Citizen* can chronicle a flowing oil well at Raton. Dr. J.J. Shuler is the president of the Raton Oil Company with C.N. Blackwell, the banker, as treasurer and George W. Earnshaw, secretary.

"Mr. Hall is enthusiastic over the outlook for the Raton Oil Company and predicts a big gusher will soon be tapped."

Prior to Mr. Hall's report to Colorado investors, several Raton citizens, including Dr. J. J. Shuler and Dr. H. B. Hayden had formed The New Mexico Land, Oil and Development Company that would own and control thousands of acres of what appeared to be oil rich land. Then they formed the Raton Oil and Gas Company as the operating company.

The $15,000 in the bank was derived from the sale of stock issued at a penny a share. Half of the stock was sold to investors in Colorado Springs and Raton investors purchased the remaining half. On May 8, 1902 *The Gazette*, a Raton newspaper, reported:

"The Raton oil stock is booming – if you don't believe it just try to buy some. Stock is eagerly sought at 100 per cent advance, but most of our people know when they have a good thing and are content to hold awhile. The oil business has created the best general spirit among our people that has been felt for years…The indications for oil are unquestionably splendid and the indication of boring at one site are unquestioned. The feeling prevails that we have oil in paying quantities which only awaits the driller."

On July 4th the work of drilling the first oil well in the Raton field began. That day *The Gazette*, reported, "At this writing the well is down 2163 feet. Oil seepage was encountered at a depth of about 400 feet and has been in evidence the remainder of the distance bored. Experts say that the probabilities of an early strike of the oil in the well are very favorable and express the utmost confidence in the success of the operating company."

The excitement spread and a second company was soon incorporated. It was called The Northern New Mexico Crude Oil Company and consisted of businessmen from Raton. The capital stock was $350,000, divided into seven million shares with a par value of five cents a share. How many shares of the stock were actually sold is unknown.

The number of wells drilled is also unknown. However, all these test wells were dry. After a period of time, when all funds were exhausted, it became obvious that the search for oil in the Raton area was a failure. Investors lost all of their money and there were cries of swindle. To this day no one really knows if the oil venture was a scam or simply a business venture that failed.

Epilog

It is probable that the search for oil was a business venture that failed. Drs. Shuler and Hayden continued their practice in Raton. Dr. Shuler was so popular that when our theatre was built in 1914 it was named in his honor.

In 1999 PennzEngery and Sonat E&P entered into a joint venture to began drilling hundreds of natural gas wells on the Vermejo Park property, located west of Raton. They are reported to have found trillions of cubic feet of natural gas in the methane coal beds, but still they found no oil.

Theater in Raton

Raton citizens have enjoyed live theater since 1880 when the city boasted a theater that attracted road shows on a regular basis. Around 1882 an opera house, known as the Old Rink, was erected. Pictured below, it was said to have "Held social sway on Second Street."

At one time Raton had five theaters. One, named The Lyric, featured a three-piece orchestra to accompany its early silent movies. Another was The Grand that hosted concerts, stock companies, boxing, wrestling and lectures. And there was The Princess that, like the Lyric, catered to products of the film industry.

In 1912, the largest theatre in New Mexico was Raton's Coliseum which could seat 5000 patrons.

Raton History Mystery and More

Then came Hugo Seaburg's Garden Coliseum. It was the largest theater in all of New Mexico at the time. It was an enormous wooden structure that could seat 5,000 patrons, which was roughly the equivalent of the entire population of Raton. Unfortunately, the Coliseum burned to the ground in 1912. Its destruction laid the groundwork for construction of what was to become the Shuler Auditorium.

The Shuler Auditorium (above) was the product of a far-sighted city council led by Mayor Dr. John Jackson Shuler. The council's original plan was to build a modest City Hall with $25,000 that had been voted on by the taxpayers for the purpose. But destruction of the Coliseum had left Raton without a large major theater. The city council decided to enlarge the original plan and include, besides an auditorium, a fire station, extra office space, jail, and a heating plant large enough to heat the jail which was located next door.

Architect William Rapp of Trinidad was hired to design the new building. It was to be patterned after municipal buildings throughout Europe. The auditorium was to conform to the classic opera house formula, including opera boxes. Its decoration, designed by F. Mayer, was to be representatve of the 18th Century European style Rococo.

As with any public project, public support waned but all was overcome and the cornerstone was laid in August of 1914.

Dr. Shuler died in 1919. The City Council, as a tribute to Dr. Shuler, passed a resolution that stated, "Now, therefore, in recognition of such services, be it Resolved, that the said municipal auditorium be hereafter known and designated on the records of the city as the Shuler Auditorium."

Raton History Mystery and More

The Shuler Auditorium has hosted thousands of events over the years. More detailed information can be obtained by reading the booklet "The Shuler Auditorium" written by Ken Sandelin. Tours of the Auditorium are available by reservation.

Visitors to Raton should take time to view the eight wonderful panel murals on the ceiling in the Shuler Foyer. Artist Manville Chapman painted them when funding was available under the PWAP Project during the depression years. The scenes portray some of the history of Raton and surrounding communities. The murals are as follows:

- *Cheyenne Village* represents the annual spring buffalo hunts. The mural shows William Bent, who married a Cheyenne Princess, and Ceran St. Vrain, who came from European royalty.
- *Wooten Toll Gate*, as built by "Uncle Dick Wooten," was the first good, passable road to Raton over the mountains. Charges to use the Toll Road were 50¢ per wagon; 25¢ per man on horseback; and 10¢ a head for livestock. Indians could use the road at no charge.
- *Willow Springs Ranch* was a resting place for tired travelers after crossing Raton Pass. The ranch originally served as a forage station because it had a deep spring with ample water.
- *Clifton Station*, located about six miles southwest of Raton, was where the early Barlow and Sanderson stagecoaches stopped. It was a two-story building that had six sleeping rooms and its own cemetery.
- *Maxwell's Mansion* is a view of a house given to Carlos Beaubien and Guadalupe Miranda by Governor Manuel Armijo. It was part of the nearly two-million-acre Maxwell Land Grant.
- *Elizabethtown* was a gold mining community located between the communities of Eagle Nest and Red River. The town was surveyed in 1867 and officially became the county seat in 1868. "E" town, as it was commonly called, is now a ghost town.
- *Raton First Street* depicts scenes from around 1893. Some of the buildings were built as early as 1880. The town was officially mapped in 1891.
- *Blossburg Mine* was located about five miles northwest of Raton and began operations in 1881. The Raton Coal & Coking Comhe Santa Fe Railroad owned the town jointly. Blossburg once claimed a population of over a thousand people.

Note: When viewing these murals, notice that Artist Chapman has one figure in each mural point, with the left arm, toward the following mural.

In the 1940's the Shuler, with its restored marquee, was the site of Raton's living Christmas tree and civic decorations.

The City of Bethlehem

Every year around Christmas, the Climax Canyon area on the Western outskirts of Raton bursts into a brilliant display of biblical scenes that include the baby Jesus, Joseph and Mary, the three Wise Men, numerous angels and much, much more. It takes thousands of light bulbs and nearly 300 man-hours of work each year to erect the holiday display that has been called "The City of Bethlehem."

A must-see for any yuletide visitor to Raton, The City of Bethlehem has been featured in numerous publications including *New Mexico Magazine*, as well as several television broadcasts by New Mexico television stations.

It all started in 1946 with a house painter named Woody Ballard who was also a talented artist. Ballard's idea for a nativity scene for Raton was borrowed from Madrid, New Mexico, where the "Nativity Lights of Madrid" originated in the former coal-mining town located about 24 miles southwest of Santa Fe. During the Christmas season thousands of visitors went to view the town's elaborate Christmas display. Over 40 thousand electric bulbs were used to light up the town. On the adjacent mountainsides were life-size figures depicting numerous biblical scenes.

When World War II broke out, the displays were discontinued and stored in a warehouse. The citizens of Madrid hoped that after the war the displays would once again transform Madrid into the Yuletide fairyland that had made it famous. Unfortunately, the warehouse that stored the Christmas lights was destroyed by fire and everything was lost. Neither the lights of Madrid nor the figures lost in the fire were ever replaced.

In the meantime, Ballard created a small nativity scene that was constructed of cutout plywood and placed it on the front lawn of the Colfax County Court House. His creation was an instant success. In fact, the nativity scene became so popular that it was enlarged and relocated to Climax Canyon located in the western outskirts of Raton.

Ballard, an active member of the Raton Lions Club, persuaded the club to help enlarge the Climax Canyon scenes. A drive to raise funds was successful. Ballard and the Lions Club eventually erected several more nativity sets.

Raton History Mystery and More

In 1952 the entire display was moved to a location along the Old Raton Pass road where more scenes were added. However, the Old Pass Road presented many problems. Traffic on the road became dangerous, especially when the weather was bad. Nor were there poles on which to attach the neccesary wiring needed to light the displays. After two years the Lions Club decided to move the City of Bethlehem back to its Climax Canyon location, where it has remained to this day.

To encourage children to visit the City of Bethlehem a series of Toyland displays were added in late 1960's. The City of Bethlehem now consists of more than 50 individual characters and biblical scenes. Permanent steel mountings have been installed for the scenes. Funds for maintaining the City of Bethlehem come from private donations and fund raising activities by the Lions Club.

Electricity to light the displays is furnished by Raton Public Service at no charge. The Raton Kiwanis Club allows the use of their Boy Scout Hut located in the canyon as home for the operators who furnish the music and maintain the scenes.

If you are in the Raton area during the Christmas holidays, make it a point to visit the Lion's Club City of Bethlehem.

Raton's Business Community
1929 and 1949

Change is inevitable, particularly in a community's business center. I thought it might be interesting and fun for young and old, as well as newcomers to Raton, to see what businesses were located in Raton years ago. Let's take a quick look at some of the city's establishments of 1929.

Automobiles

If you were in the market for a Durant automobile you would go to the Liberty Garage at 200 South Second. Perhaps you preferred an Oakland or Pontiac. Then you would visit Nigro & Donati's located at 312 North Second. If you had your heart set on a Studebaker or Erskine, you would shop Van Dyke Motor Company at 210 South Second. To see the USA in a Chevrolet, Sunshine Chevrolet Co. at 210 South Second was the place to go.

Central Garage at 219 North Second sold Chrysler, and Davis Garage at the corner of Second and Rio Grande sold Buick. Gate City Garage at 201 North Second had any style Dodge you wanted.

You could finance your car at General Finance Company, 211 Park Avenue, First National Bank, 130 Park Ave., International State Bank, 144 South Second; or the National Bank of New Mexico, located at 114 Park Ave. If your car broke down, there were at least 11 garages that could fix it. Nine were located on Second Street. If the car needed a new paint job for any reason, Raton Sign and Duco Shop, 428 North Fourth, could do the job. If you needed a new auto top, B & L Auto Shop, 222 Clark Ave., was the place to go. You knew the automobile was here to stay when the only place you could get horseshoes for your horse was Cassell's Blacksmith Shop located at 325 Sugarite Avenue.

Main Street, now Second, photographed about 1922.

And again in 1940.

Bakeries

There were four bakeries in 1929. Quality Bakery was located at 125 Cook Avenue and Raton Bakery baked their goodies at 130 North Second. Two of the bakeries were located on Garcia Street. One was the Sunshine Bakery and the other was named White Lily Bakery.

Clothing and Dry Goods

Clothing and dry good stores were plentiful. Located on First Street were The Golden Rule Store at 124 South First, Louis Maio and Son located at 224 South First; and Price Shoe & Clothing Company that occupied the building at 140 North First.

There were several clothing and dry goods stores on Second Street. Among them were The Golden Eagle located at 113 South Second, Kilmurray Clothing Co. located at 100 South Second, Raton Commercial Company at 142 South Second, and J.C. Penny, which was housed at 125 South Second. H. C. Fordyce & Company occupied the corner at Second and Cook and Johnson Clothing Company was at 8 Cook Avenue.

Ladies could buy the latest fashions and millinery at Engledow Toggery located at 136 North Second, The Style Shop at 136 South Second, Morgan Bonnet and Needlework Shoppe at 209 Park Avenue, Rose Striker at 133 Park Avenue, or H. C. Fordyce at the corner of second and Cook.

Furniture and General Merchandise

If you needed new furniture for your home, you could shop W.H. Boan, 112 North First, Tomlinson Furniture Co., 225 South Second, or F.A. Walker at 120 North First Street.

General Merchandise was available from Azar Brothers located at the corner of Cook and Martinez Streets or Colfax Mercantile Company at 129 Cook Avenue. The Leader at 132 South First and C. DiMarzio located at 208 First Street also sold general merchandise.

Grocery Stores

There were no big super markets in 1929. However, there were 20 independent grocers where you could buy your groceries. A few that may bring back fond memories to some of our senior citizens are Blue Front Grocery, Community Grocery, Fulton Market, Payne Grocery, Piggly Wiggly, Prince's Grocery, Snodgrass Food Company, and Peter Yob, who had a dandy little shop located at 138 South First.

Candy and Ice Cream Shops

Since this was a year of prohibition, there were no bars, at least not legally! Since people couldn't drink, they must have eaten a lot of candy and ice cream because besides the Sweet Shop, three additional ice cream and confectionery stores existed. They were The Blue Parrot at 123 North Second, J.M. and V.C. Honeyfield at 145 Cook, and Pete Johnson at 123 North Second.

Restaurants

There were at least 15 restaurants that served a wide variety of foods. You could choose from any of the following: Annie's Spanish Café, Bon Ton Café, Boston Lunch, The Coffee Shop, Corona Café, DeLuxe Café, Highway Sandwich Shop, J. R. Leson, Manhattan Café, McIntosh's Restaurant, The Oasis, The Silver Moon Café, Swastika Café, Frank Valentino, and the White Front Lunch.

Diamonds and Stationary

Diamonds and jewelry were available at C.A. Whited and Son or Velhagen Brothers. Office supplies and stationary as well as film and cameras were available at Sandusky's located at 117 South Second.

Medical

If you needed medical attention you could call any of the following doctors: Dr. Richard Fuller, Dr. H.W. Heymann, Dr. Thomas Lyon, Dr. W.E.Rice, Dr. M.F.Smith, Dr. A.B.Stewart, Dr. Whitcomb, or Dr. Elliott, They even made house calls in 1929. Prescriptions were filled at A.J.Lambert's, Nutting Drug Store or Raton Drug Company.

Cook Avenue, facing east toward the railroad station.

Raton History Mystery and More

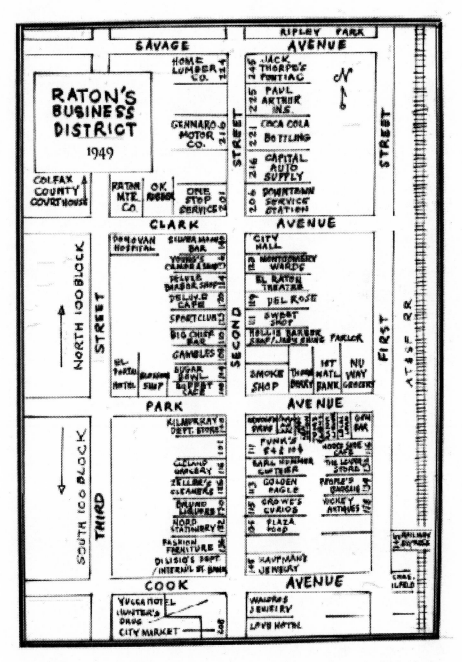

Jim Mulling's map of the 1949 business area gives a general view of where many of the 1949 businesses were located. The map is not to scale and because of the complexity of such a drawing, we're not even 100% certain we have it right. But we're very close!

Raton History Mystery and More

Twenty Years Later - 1949

Now, let's take a look at a portion of the business community in 1949. In this section I am listing the name of the business and its address on a block-by-block basis. Even "Street" numbers are on the west side of the street, odd numbers are on the east side of the street.For "Avenue" addresses, the even numbers are on the north side of the avenue and odd numbers are on the south side. Park Avenue divides north from south. Any address north of Park Avenue starts as 100 north. Addresses south of Park Avenue start as 100 south.

The reason for this listing is because every year I meet many relatives; second, third, and even fourth generations, of the owners of these businesses. They ask me if I knew where their parents, grandparents, or great-grand parents had their business or where they worked. In other words, this part of my story is to help people locate a part of their family history.

North First Street
- 100 - NuWay Market
- 110 - Raton Shoe Shop
- 112 - Savoy Liquor Store
- 132 - Raton Coal Company

South First Street
- 100 - Gem Bar
- 116 - Horse Shoe Café
- 132 - The Leader Store
- 134 - People's Bargain Store
- 138 - Hickey Antique Shop
- 145 - Railway Express Agency
- 220 - Windle Second Hand Store
- 325 - Charles Ilfeld Company
- 329 - Santa Fe Beverage Company

North Second Street
- 100 - Buffet Bar
- 101 - Joe's Shine Parlor
- 104 - Sally's Sugar Bowl
- 107 - Hollis Barber Shop
- 108 - Gambles
- 111 - The Sweet Shop
- 114 - Big Chief Bar
- 118 - Sport Club
- 119 - Del Rose Shop
- 120 - Deluxe Café

North Second Street (Continued)

123 - Montgomery Ward

124 - Deluxe Barber Shop

136 -Young's Camera Shop

140 - Silver Moon Café

200 - Down Town Service Station

201 - One Stop Service Station

212 - Capital Auto Supply

216 - Gennaro Motor Company

221 - Coca-Cola Bottling Company

224 - Home Lumber Company

225 - Paul Arthur Motor Company

228 - Norman Motor Parts Company

245 - Jack Thorp Pontiac Company

301 - Raton Public Library

314 - Raton Wholesale Liquor Company

South Second Street

100 - Kilmurray Clothing

101 - Funk's Five & Ten Cent Store

111 - Earl Hummer's Men Wear

113 - Golden Eagle

115 - Crowe's Jewelry and Gift Shop

116 - Cleland's Grocery Store

126 - Northern New Mexico Gas Company

126 - Zeller's Cleaners

130 - Bruno Liquor Store

132 - Nord Stationery Store

135 - Plaza Food Store

136 - Fashion Furniture

145 - Kaufman's Jewelry

200 - Hunter's Drug Store

203 - Waldron Jewelry

205 - Love Hotel

208 - City Market

217 - Greyhound Curio Shop

245 - City Taxi Company

Clark Avenue:
> 124 - Keeter Car Market
> 209 - OK Rubber Welders
> 245 - Donovan's Hospital
> 246 - Raton Motor Company

Park Avenue
> 125 - Park Avenue Café
> 127 - Western Union
> 129 - Thomas Plumbing & Heating
> 131 - Raton Liquor Store
> 133 - Local Loan Company
> 142 - Petite Gift Shop
> 144 - Clements & Stafford Barber Shop
> 146 - Smoke Shop
> 205 - Brown's Paint & Glass Shop
> 209 - City Shoe Shop
> 214 - Blossom Flower Shop

When you wanted to call one these businesses, you picked up the telephone and spoke with a real live telephone operator. Home phones were usually party lines for which the number ended with a letter such as J, R, W, and so forth. I still remember my old home phone number; 419-R. Businesses were lucky and usually had a private line that did not end with a letter. The old Sweet Shop's phone number was 680. I hope many of you who may have had parents, grandparents, or great-grandparents managing or owning any of these businesses enjoyed this tour down memory lane.

Coal Camps of Colfax County

While I was growing up in Raton one of the highlights during the year was when my parents loaded the car with my two brothers and myself and headed for one of the coal camps to celebrate a special occasion. The occasion could have been a birthday, a holiday, a wedding, a baptism, or just a weekend outing.

We always ended up in "Greek Town," the cluster of homes that housed most of the Greeks who lived there. We had Greek friends in nearly every coal camp: The Maverdakis, Boukitis, and Scandalis in Dawson, the Kalamani's in Van Houten, and the Christos in Sugarite, to name a few.

Most of the coal camp's residents clustered by nationalities because of language barriers, not color or religion. Besides Greek Town, there was Italian Town, Mexican Town and other clusters that housed Chinese and African Americans. The reason, of course, was because most of these people were immigrants and few spoke English. What little English was known was incomplete and usually used only when conversing with mine bosses and shopkeepers.

Coal miners were hard working people who sweated, toiled, shoveled, lifted, and hauled coal for a living. The housewives maintained the home, shopped for food and clothing and, naturally, raised the children. Everyone worked hard to make coal camp life as normal as possible.

The largest coal camp in Colfax County was Dawson and that was the town we visited most often. I could probably write an entire book on the days I spent at Dawson playing with my friends, laughing at the Greeks who got drunk and homesick for the homeland, and stuffing myself with all the homemade Greek food and *pastriesm* those wonderful Greek mothers baked for their families. But, since this is basically a book on history, I thought readers might enjoy learning a little about life in Dawson at the turn of the century.

Dawson's population in 1909 was 4,000 people of which 1,163 were coal miners. Besides the underground coal mines, Dawson had 570 coke ovens in operation. This included 124 beehive ovens that were 13 feet in diameter. There were also 446 English under-flue ovens that measured 11 feet in diameter. Each oven was charged with six tons of slack, burned 48 hours at a time, to produce 52% of its weight in coke.

There were 594 houses, mostly company owned, containing four to eight rooms and some larger dwellings that were used for boarding and lodging houses. House rent was reasonable. A two-room house rented for $4.00 a month; a three-room house was $6.00 a month; and for those who could afford a four-room house, the rent was $8.00 a month. These rates were about one-half the going rate for rent for similar houses in other towns and cities outside the coal camps.

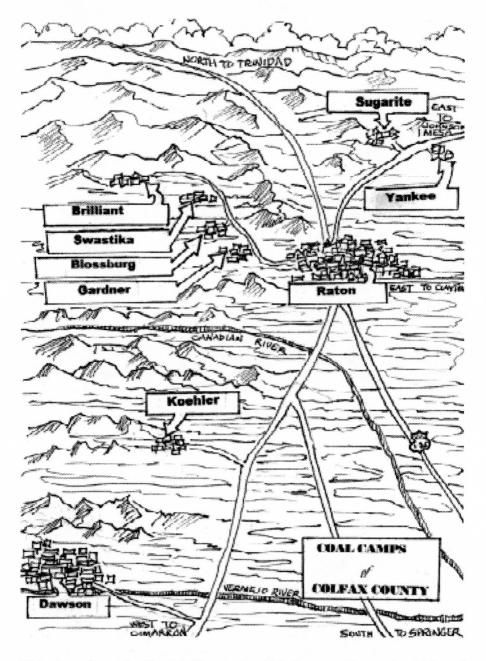

This map, drawn by Jim Mullings, should help you enjoy a visual idea of the locations of the many coal camps in Colfax County.

Electric lights cost 25¢ a month for each 16-candlepower light and 50¢ for 32-candlepower lights. Again, this was about one-half the going rate in cities outside the coal camps. Water was furnished without charge.

Wages in Dawson were good. Fire bosses made $3.25 a day. Pit bosses earned $125.00 a month. Tracklayers were paid $2.95 a day. Electricians reaped $3.50 a day. The boys that attended the doors into the mineshafts collected $1.15 a day. Carpenters wages varied from $2.75 to $4.00 per day and engineers merited $90.00 a month.

But there were payroll deductions. Miners had to pay for their own supplies. Lamp oil was 70¢ a gallon. Lamp cotton was 5¢ a ball. Powder was $2.75 a keg. Additional deductions included a hospital fee of $1.50 a month. This charge covered medicines, admission to the hospital and surgical procedures when they were necessary.

Education for the young was a must because most of these miners had little if any schooling, and they knew the importance of an education. Children of the miners could attend school in one of two large schoolhouses. The company built one and the other was paid for by the school district.

Employees paid $1.00 out of their monthly check to finance the school district. The cost to operate the schools was $12,000 for the school year. The school district budgeted $5,000 and the company appropriated enough money to make up the deficit. Dawson had a full 10-month school year. There were nine teachers, two janitors, and 445 students.

The company did many other things to improve the social life of the coal miners and their families. For example, the company built a large theatre that cost $35,000. The first floor contained the theatre and a large billiard parlor. The second floor contained the galleries of the theater and a large furnished lodge room where various societies could hold their meetings.

The Company also maintained a large general store that supplied everything from food to the necessity and luxury items that were desired by the miners and their families. All the merchandise was sold at prices comparable or lower than those charged in towns outside the coal camps. Food prices, however, were generally lower than those in other towns located in the Territory.

If the history of Dawson fascinates you, get a copy of *Coal Town, The life and Times of Dawson, New Mexico* written by Toby Smith. The book brings the every day life of the citizens of Dawson to life and dwells on everything from social functions to sports. There are also numerous photos and artifacts that can be seen at the Raton Museum.

Here are a few tidbits about the coal camps in Colfax County that you may find interesting.

- Colfax County produced over 75 percent of the coal mined in New Mexico and was the only county producing coke.
- St. Louis Rocky Mountain and Pacific Company was the largest producer of coal in the state. It had mines at Brilliant, Gardiner, Van Houten, Koehler, and Sugarite.
- In 1911 there was a scarcity of miners. The mines in Colfax County directly employed a total of 3,563 persons.
  Company rules stated that boys under 12 years of age could not work in any mine.

. In 1923, St. Louis Rocky Mountain and Pacific Company had 1712 employees. There were 280 natural born Americans, 384 natural born Spanish-Americans, 52 Negroes, and 160 naturalized citizens. In addition, there were 96 Austrians, one Belgian, 42 Britons, three Bulgarians, one Canadian, two Czechs, three Frenchmen, two Germans, 44 Greeks, 13 Hungarians, 271 Italians, 40 Japanese, 21 Yugoslavians, 121 from Mexico, 15 Montenegros, one Polish, one Russian, 12 Serbians, one miner from Turkey and one from Switzerland. Colfax County was an international melting pot.

Coal Mining and The Economy of Colfax County

The economic foundation for Raton and all neighboring communities in Colfax County was based on activities at the coal camps. If the mines were in production, the economy and social welfare of the communities was good. If the mines were closed, everyone suffered, both economically and socially. In a sense, Raton and its surrounding neighbors lived or died as a result of coal mining activities for most of the 20th century.

For example, in 1909, when New Mexico was still a territory, the coal mining communities in Colfax County produced 2,027,639 tons of coal. This was 74.85% of the total tonnage of new coal mined in the Territory of New Mexico. Yet, times were not good.

Market prices for coal were down. Oil strikes in Texas and Oklahoma curtailed the demand for coal from New Mexico mines by 30%. To make matters worse, in 1908 the Mexican Government had taken over the ownership of the Mexican Central Railroad and increased the freight rate by $1.00 a ton on coal shipped from El Paso to the smelters at Monterey. Most of this coal came from Raton-area mines.

Some mines, such as the Yankee mine, had to close down because of financial problems. Many other mines, while financially stable, were only active for six or seven months of the year. Yet, for reasons unknown, Colfax County increased its production of coal. It was estimated that 5 million tons of coal could be produced annually, even with the economic uncertainties of those days.

Summary

Life in the coal camps was hard, but rewarding. The miners and their families lived in harmony and worked well together. They enjoyed life. There was no welfare. They took care of each other. There were no homeless because the miners took in total strangers and found work for them. Divorce was frowned upon.

Today, all of the coal camps are gone and only a few foundations and perhaps a smoke stack or two remain. Every year the former citizens of Dawson and their descendants hold a reunion around Labor Day. Many of the other camps also have reunions on occasion. The memories of the coal camps will never die because, truly, the coal camps of Colfax County were and are something to behold.

In 1906 (Top) Dawson was a large and well-established coal mining community. The largest building in town (Bottom) was the Opera House, beyond which are the coke ovens and railroad.

The Dawson Hotel (Top) was owned and operated by the coal company. The Opera House (Bottom), photographed in 1909, was the center of many activities for the families of Dawson.

A Quick Look At Some Of The Other Coal Mines In Colfax County

While Dawson was the largest, and probably the most active coal mine in Colfax County, there were numerous other mines that are worthy of mention.

Koehler 1919

Koehler was located about 16 miles southwest of Raton in what was called Prairie Crow Canyon. Koehler was owned by The St. Louis, Rocky Mountain and Pacific Company and began its mining operations around 1906. More than a thousand people once claimed Koehler as their home. The town had a two-story school, its own electric generating plant, post office, doctor's office, several stores, and three boarding houses where many of the miners lived. Koehler closed in 1924, but got a second chance in 1936, when the coal mines reopened.

Kaiser Steel eventually purchased the property, but Koehler, as a coal-mining town, ceased to exist and is now a ghost town.

Gardner

Coal production began in Gardner in 1882. The Raton Coal and Coke Company operated Gardiner in conjunction with the St. Louis, Rocky Mountain and Pacific Company. The town was located about three miles west of Raton. Gardiner had a modern hospital staffed by two doctors and five nurses as well as several businesses.

At one time there were over 300 coke ovens (Above) in Gardiner. The mines were closed in 1939, but some activity continued during World War II. In 1954 the machine shop finally closed and Gardner joined the list of mining ghost towns. While there are a few remains, the camp is closed to the public.

Sugarite 1915

Sugarite was established in 1912 and was developed by the Chicorica Coal Company. The mine was located in Chicorica Canyon about seven miles north of Raton. Eventually it was taken over by the St. Louis, Rocky Mountain and Pacific Company. In 1915, there were 500 people living in the Sugarite area.

The town had a school, post office, opera house, boarding house, and company store. As in most coal camps, the town had several privately owned businesses and bars. There was also a Justice of the Peace, music teacher and an office of the Bell Telephone Company.

The St. Louis, Rocky Mountain and Pacific Company announced the closing of Sugarite in 1941. By 1944, all that remained were the ruins that you can still see today as you drive to Lake Maloya. Today, Sugarite is a New Mexico State Park, managed by the State of New Mexico.

Blossburg

Blossberg opened in 1881 and was jointly owned by the Raton Coal and Coking Company and the Santa Fe Railroad. It was located about five miles northwest of Raton.

Blossburg once claimed over a thousand residents. However, a series of strikes, and numerous labor problems contributed to Blossburg's short life. There were only 100 persons remaining in 1903 and that figure dwindled to about 20 people by 1939. Today, Blossburg has joined the list of coal mining ghost towns. This photo shows Blossburg when it had hundreds of residents. The exact date of the photo is not known, but museum officials believe it was taken in the late 1880's.

The St. Louis, Rocky Mountain and Pacific Company

The St. Louis, Rocky Mountain and Pacific Company, organized in 1905, owned many of the coal camps in Colfax County. The company opened the first coal mine named Brilliant in 1906. The name Brilliant referred to the sheen of coal from Tin Pan Canyon. It had a high luster superior to most coal. The Brilliant coal seams were located about seven miles northwest of Raton.

Within one year, the population totaled 350 people. Swastika and Brilliant are often confused as one and the same town. Brilliant and Swastika actually functioned side by side.

The original Brilliant closed about 1935 and only Swastika remained. Because of World War II with Germany, it became obvious that Swastika was not an appropriate name. Swastika was then renamed Brilliant II.

Swastika

By 1929, Swastika's population was 500 residents. Growth occurred because the oil boom in Texas and Oklahoma required large amounts of coal that was converted to steam power, which in turn drove the rotary drills used in the oil fields. The town of Swastika, that had been renamed Brilliant II, was closed in 1954.

Van Houten

Van Houten, also owned by the St. Louis, Rocky Mountain and Pacific Company was originally named Willow. The name Willow was changed to Van Houten in honor of the company's president, Jan Van Houten. By 1915, Van Houten had a population of about 1500 residents.

Van Houten had a company store, two hotels, a barber shop and several other businesses and several bars. There was also a stage line that transported people to Raton.

In 1948 a serious strike dealt a deathblow to Van Houten and finally in 1954, all mining activity ceased. Van Houten is now part of the site of the NRA Whittington Center. The St. Louis, Rocky Mountain and Pacific Company no longer exists.

Small, Independent Mines

There were also smaller, independently owned mines in the area. Elmer Sperry, who operated the Sperry Mine, hauled coal by horse and wagon to Raton where it was sold for domestic purposes. The Turner mine was located about 12 miles northeast of Raton. The Honeyfield mine was nine miles northeast of Raton and one mile from the Yankee mine. M. Smigelow owned the Mendelsohn mine. It was abandoned in 1913 because satisfactory railroad track was not available.

Yankee Coal Camp. Date unknown.

There are no active coal mines in Colfax County today. The last operating mine, owned by, Pittsburgh and Midway Coal Mining Company, a subsidiary of ChevronTexaco, closed its mining operations in June of 2002.

There are several books available about the coal camps of New Mexico. An excellent book is *Ghost Towns and Mining Camps of New Mexico* written by James E. and Barbara H. Sherman. *New Mexico's Best Ghost Towns* by Philip Varney features not only the coal mining camps, but also other New Mexico ghost towns of interest. Toby Smith wrote *Coal Town, The Life and Times of Dawson, New Mexico* that is full of interesting stories about the people who lived in Dawson. And the Raton Museum has a series of books about the mining towns in Colfax County written by Father Stanley

Dawson's Mine Disaster
October 22, 1913

Most of the time life at the coal camps was uneventful. The most feared, but seldom talked about concern of the coal miners and their families, was the possibility of a serious mine disaster. While there were numerous accidents and an occasional fatality, no one anticipated the mine explosion in Dawson that claimed the lives of 263 miners.

The explosion occurred about three o'clock on Wednesday afternoon, October 23, 1913 in Coal Mine No. 2 of the Stag Canyon Fuel Company. The Thursday edition of the *Raton Reporter* stated, "The cause of the explosion is not known and may never be definitely determined. This mine was supposed to be as near safe as engineering skill and money could make it and that such a terrible disaster could occur is almost beyond belief of those having full knowledge of the conditions."

Rescue crews, called "helmet men," from as far away as Rock Springs, Wyoming; Trinidad, Colorado; Kansas and Pittsburg. rushed to Dawson to aid local area mine crews in the rescue process. A United States Relief Car from Denver, Colorado was also sent to the scene of the disaster. The rescue work was slow and dangerous. Two helmet men, William Poysner and James Laird from Koehler died, apparently from suffocation, while engaged in the rescue work.

Of the 283 miners originally entombed in the shafts only 20 were brought out alive. 223 bodies were recovered and 40 bodies remained in the mine because they were unrecoverable.

"Funeral services for the dead," as reported by the *Raton Reporter*, "are being conducted from time to time by Rev. Father Cellier of Springer Catholic and by Rev. Harvey M. Shields of the Episcopal Church for his own and other protestant denominations. All through the services, which were made mercifully brief, could be heard the chanting of Austrian widows, hysterical cries of Mexican women, moans of the Greek bereaved and the sorrowful sobbing of a little group of American women who so suddenly had been bereft of their loved ones."

Financial aid for the families came from the Red Cross who established a $1,000 fund and from Phelps Dodge. The company gave each widow $1,000 and each child of the widow $100. The nearest relatives of single men received $500. In addition, many of the other coal camps and neighboring towns contributed both food and money.

.   Mining operations were resumed on October 29 at the other Dawson mines, but with greatly decreased production. The Dawson coal mines continued to operate until 1951 when all mining operations were shut down because of the lack of demand for coal. The town was then dismantled and most buildings auctioned to be moved off the mine property.

For readers who may be interested in a more technical review of what caused the mine explosion, here are excerpts of the 1913 report submitted by New Mexico State Mine Inspector Rees H. Beddow

"A week before the explosion occurred, I examined the mine carefully, and found no standing gas, either on top of the caves or in the live workings of the mine. The analysis of the air showed but nineteen-one-hundredths of one per cent of methane, which is very low for a mine of this character."

The cause of the explosion

"The explosion was caused by an over-charged shot (dynamite), fired in room No. 27 on the 9th west entry, on the No. 2 side of the mine. The coal from this shot was blown for a distance of forty feet from the working face. A great amount of wind had been developed by this shot, stirring up and igniting the coal dust and spreading from this point to all parts of the mine, with more or less force and flame, being influenced largely by the amount of water or dust it came in contact with.

"The explosion traveled with such violence as to entomb 284 miners, all of whom were killed instantly, except 14 men in the first east entry of the high-line, who were rescued by their own efforts, and nine men who were rescued at about 8 P.M. on the night of the explosion, near the bottom of the air shaft, by a rescuing party.

"These men were all unconscious, but were revived by the use of pul-motors. Two helmet men (rescue workers) were lost the night following the explosion by over-exerting themselves, and going in farther than the foreman allowed them to go."

How the explosion occurred

"The shot (that caused the explosion) was fired by a miner while all the men were in the mine. It was done by connecting his shooting wire with the trolley wire, which is against the company's rules, and in violation of the State mining laws. The company had provided a separate system of wires for blasting, which is protected by three cutout switches. The current was not allowed to be turned on to these wires until all of the men were out of the mine. However, the miner wanted to load a few more cars of coal that day, so he took a chance by connecting on to the trolley wire, fired a shot while all the men were in the mine, and started an explosion that cost him his life, and 263 others suffered the same fate.

"The mine was a modern one in every respect. The ventilating system was well planned, the equipment was first class and the shot firing system as planned by the company, can not be beaten."

The effects of coal dust

The report further discussed the problem with coal dust. The dust is carried by air currents and settles on the walls and timbers along the entryways. According to the mine inspector's report, coal dust will also settle "In quiet places where the air current is not so strong, and in this dust lies the greatest danger to the operation the mines."

The report also stated, "The amount of coal dust necessary to propagate an explosion throughout a mine is a debatable question, upon which there is some difference of opinion. It has been demonstrated by the U.S. Bureau of Mines, that as low as .248 of an ounce of coal dust to the cubic foot of gallery or entry, up to .568 of an ounce, is sufficient to propagate an explosion.

"It appears to me," the mine inspector continued, "That just so long as we have so many inexperienced men working in the mines, and they be allowed to handle, charge, tamp and fire their own shots, we will have mine explosions."

How true those last lines of Beddow's report were. Ten years later, on February 8, 1923, the nearby Stag Canyon No. 1 had an explosion that killed 120 miners. For history buffs, the three worst coal mine disasters in U.S. history were the 1907 Monongah, West Virginia, mine explosion that killed 362 miners, the 1913 Dawson mine explosion that killed 263 miners and the Cherry, Illinois, mine fire that killed 259 miners.

Dawson is now a ghost town, but memories of the tragedy of the 1913 explosion can be vividly demonstrated by visiting the cemetery at Dawson. It has been well maintained over the years and is just a short walk from the end of the road leading to Dawson.

Following are names of miners who died in that 1913 explosion as listed in the Mine Inspectors of New Mexico, Second Annual Report. As you read the list, notice how many family members were lost.

A

John Amargiotu, Greek
John Anastasakis, Greek
John Andres, Greek
Pavlo Andres, Greek
Thelfano Andrios, Greek
Makis Anezakis, Greek
Stilen Anezakis, Greek
Michele Angela, Italian
Pete Angelone, Italian
Nick Arkotas, Greek
Rocco Armeda, Italian

B

Battista Ballastrocci, Italian
Antonio Bediali, Italian
Celeste Bediali, Italian
Angelo Bella, Italian
Jerry Berger, American
Giovanni Biagio, Italian
Silvestre Biagio, Italian
Gugliemo Bianchi, Italian
Luigi Biondi, Italian
Pietro Boggio, Italian
Dom Bonnio, Italian
Anton Bono, Italian
Nick Bouzakis, Greek
Guiseppi Bravieri, Italian
Willis Bright, Negro
J.M. Brooks, Negro
Frank Brown, Negro
Domenic Brugione, Italian
Federico Brugione, Italian
Listo Brugione, Italian
Vanni Brugione, Italian
Joe Brunos, Italian
Edward Butte, Italian

C

Antonia Comacho, Mexican
Demaretio Candido, Italian
Guiseppi Carapello, Italian
B. Carapellucci, Italian
D. Carapellucci, Italian
Guiseppi, Careto, Italian
Carlo Carlesco, Italian
John Carlesco, Italian
Antonio Carrole, Italian
Magus Castenagus, Greek
Ermenegildo Castelli, Italian
Giovanni Cavaiani, Italian,
John Cericola, Italian
Mazoli Cerillo, Italian
R. Champa Austrian
Luis Chavez, Mexican
Marcial Chavez, Mexican
Pietro Cecconi, Italian
Ubaldo Ciccarelli, Italian
John Colonintes, Greek
A. Conti, Italian
Mike Coral, Slav
Geo. Cotrules, Greek
Mak Cotrules, Greek
F. Cruz, Mexican
Giovanni Curioroni, Italian

D

A. Daen, American
Pietro Dalzotto, Italian
J. F. Davis, Negro
C. N. Davis, American
Niclo DiCicco, Italian
Giocomo Dellaca, Italian
Joe DeMichelli, Italian
Luigii Dianna, Italian
Guiseppe DiPaulo, Italian
Romono Duica, Italian

E-F

Ed Egar, Mexican
Authur English, American
B. Enrico, Italian
Chas. Evans, Negro
Nicolo Fabba, Italian
Chas. Farriano, Italian
Michael Fanarakis, Greek
John Farrina, Italian
Geo. Fauri, Italian
A. Fideli, Italian
Bart Foglia, Italian

G

Anselmo Gabrelli, Italian
Dan Gallegos, Mexican
Gio Ganoitt, Italian
Felipe Garcia, Mexican
Attilio Garzanillo, Italian
Killo Gatti, Italian
Gabriel Gubelick, Bohemian
Luigi Guiatto, Italian
Johaly Gulvas, Slav
J. C. Gunnoe, American
Frederico Giovanni, Italian
Pietro Grimaldo, Italian
Camello Giganti, Italian
Ernest Giancreli, Italian
Umberto Giordani, Italian
Antonio Giovanni, Italian
Geo. Gelas, Greek.

H-I-J-K

C.I. Hicks, Negro
A. Huerena, Mexican
Demetrius Iconome, Greek
Franciso Mandato, Italian
John Janos, Hungarian
John B. Jan, French

John Jessor, Russian
Walter Johnson, Negro
Wm. Kluckinsky, Russian
S.J.Krifer, American
Gust Katis, Greek
Jacob Kiefer, Hugarian
Joe Kinter, Slav

L

Vassilias Ladis, Greek
Guiseppe Ladurini, Italian
Tony Lardi, Italian
Jas. Lindsay, American
Robt. Littlejohn, American
Atilio Locci, Italian
Ben Loger, American
Gaetano Lolli, Italian
Magus Lopakis, Greek
B. Lopez, Mexican
Guiseppe Lori, Italian
Paulo Lucini, Italian

M

Iva McCutcheon, Scotch
Wm. McDermott, Irish
Alex McDonald, American
J.W.McGraw, American
Thos. McLennon, American
H.P.McShane, American
Chas. Mafiola, Italian
Vassos Magglis, Greek
Luigi Marinucci, Italian
C.E.Mahoney, American
Cost Makris, Greek
Geo. Makris, Greek
Baldo Marchetti, Italian
Fidencio Marez, Mexican

M (Continued)

John Martinelli, Italian
Victor Martinelli, Italian
Angelo Mascognon, Italian
Giacopmo Mascognon, Itl.
Frank Mati, Italian
J.W.Maxy, American
Aurelia Mazzoli, Italian
Adamo Mazzoni, Italian
Aristide Melone, Italian
Allino Menopace, Italian
Jas. Mercer, Italian
Harry Merner, American
Ermete Mesini, Italian
Marion Mesini, Italian
Alex Michael, Greek
Agosinio Micheletti, Italian
Tones Mifinigaun, Greek
Pedro Mijares, Mexican
Jno. Miklovcic, Slav
Emm Minotaties, Greek
Marcos Montanez, Mexican
Luigi Montman, Italian
Silvio Montorsi,Italian
Felix Montoya, Mexican
Nestor Montoya, Mexican
Val Montoya, Mexican
Wm. Morgan, American

N-O

O. Nardini, Italian
Antonio Natali, Italian
Guiseppe Nava, Italian
Jose Negete, Mexican
Nick Nicolocchi, Greek
Giovanni Nizzi, Italian
Andy Ola, Hungarian

P

Cost Papas, Greek
Makis Papas, Greek
Strat Papas, Greek
Sidney Prevost, Italian
Herbert Prussing, American
Giacomo Passotta, Italian
Mike Paperi, Greek
Manon Parashas, Greek
J.J. Pascoe, American
Louis Pastore, Italian
Thos. Pattison, American
Selvino Pascetta, Italian
Nicol Pascetta, Italian
Joshua Pearce, American
P. Pellegrini, Italian
Stefano Pensato, Italian
Lucciano Perez, Mexican
Dominic Pessetto, Italian
Tom Pessetto, Italian
Kros Pino, Greek
Giovanni Piros, Italian
Joe Pland, Italian
Egildo Poretti, Italian

R

Carol Ramuno, Italian
Frank Redlich, American
Wm. Redpath, American
Jesus Reyes, Mexican
A. Rifosco, Italian
Juan Ribera, Mexican
Pedro Rodriquez, Mexican
Val Roje, Austrian
Daniel Romero, Mexican
Marcelino Romero,
Mexiccan
Saturno Romolo, Italian
John Rounds, American

S

Angelo Santi, Italian
Benianio Santi, Italian
Carlo Santi, Italian
Dom. Santi, Italian
Egisto Santi, Italian
Geriomine Santi, Italian
Luigi Santi, Italian
Petro Santi, Italian
Pit Della Santi, Italian
Raymondo Santi, Italian
M. Santisteven, Mexican
Nick Saturno, Italian
Higinio Saucedo, Mexican
John Sexot, Greek
Anselmo Scrafini, Italian
Joe Serrano, Mexican
McKinley Short, American
Monfredino Silvio, Italian
Enrico Simoncini, Italian
Fritz Sitko, American
Pete Sporer, Slav
Sebastian Sporer, Slav
Frank Stafford, American
Joe Stark, Pole
Stavakis Polikronis, Greek
Jakob Subart, Slav

T

Dom Tassi, Italian
Guiseppi Tollere, Italian
Giacomo Tomasi, Italian
Pietro Tomasi, Italian
Frank Torok, Hungarian
Juan Trujillo, Mexican
Wm. Tumen, Slav
Peter Tunney, American

U-V-W-X-Y-Z

Patricio Ulibarri, Mexican
L.P.Upton, American
Ernest Vallette, Italian
Cesare Vegniti, Italian
Vic Velasco, Mexican
Antonios Vidalakis, Greek
Henry Wesley, Negro
Geo. H. Williams, Negro
J. Williams, American
Frank Wilmoth, American
J.H.Wright, American
Camillo Zacayinno, Italian
Duile Zamboni, Italian
Narcisco Zamboni, Italian
Aleide Zamboni, Italian
Andre Zandi, Italian
B. Zeffrini, Italian

Most Violent Day In Raton's History
The Story of Gus Mentzer

Gus Mentzer was one of Raton's most notorious gamblers and meanest drunks. And by the time an angry lynch mob chased him through the streets of Raton and hung him from the bank's signpost. He had caused the death of four good men.

Mentzer had come to Raton as a bartender in the Bank Exchange Saloon. William Burbridge, owner of the saloon, had met Mentzer in Texas and they became friends. When a drunk challenged Burbridge to a fight, he refused. Mentzer accepted the challenge to uphold his friend's honor and killed the drunk. Both men eventually moved to Raton. Burbridge, to show his thanks to Mentzer, hired him as a bartender. But Mentzer became a heavy gambler and a drunk, so Burbridge fired him.

On Monday June 26, 1882, Mentzer returned to the Saloon to ask Burbridge to take him back. He wouldn't and Mentzer challenged his friend to a dual. Mentzer backed out on the street with a gun in his hand to make his point. That's when the trouble began.

Deputy Sheriff R.P. Dollman was walking south on Railroad Avenue after taking a prisoner to jail minutes earlier when a half-drunk Mentzer met him with his pistol in his hand. Mentzer pointed his gun at Dollman. "Give up your gun," Dollman said. "I can't do that," replied Mentzer, and jabbed his six-gun into Dollman's side.

According to published reports, Mentzer was about to pull the trigger a nearby spectator grabbed Mentzer's arm and forced it downward. The gun went off drilling a hole in the wood boardwalk. Mentzer then wrenched himself free from the spectator, ran into the Bank Exchange Saloon and out the back door. Meanwhile, Dollman had his six-gun ready for action and fired several shots after the fleeing assailant. It is unknown if Mentzer was hit by any of the bullets. In any case, Mentzer made good his escape.

By nine o'clock Mentzer had a few hours to sober up. He returned to the Bank Exchange to have a drink and try to talk to Burbridge again. When he entered the saloon a fellow gambler named Turner greeted him. Turner was jealous of the Bank Exchange Saloon's gambling success and mad at Burbridge because he had refused to make Turner a partner. Turner wanted to see Mentzer kill Burbridge.

The Bank Exchange, a highly successful gambling hall and bar.

It is not clear how or why the shootings began but Mentzer had no sooner ordered a drink when bullets were flying all over from the back of the saloon. Mentzer shot back quickly by emptying his six-gun. Turner saw an opportunity and handed Mentzer his two pistols. But Mentzer did not want to fight it out. Instead, he ran out the door followed by a hail of bullets.

Still partly drunk and scared, Mentzer ran across the street to an open area near the railroad section house. Just as he reached the platform a man named J.H. Latimer, for some unknown reason, drew his pistol and fired at Mentzer. Mentzer fired back, wounding Latimer in the left knee and upper chest. A stray bullet also wounded a man named Harris.

Mentzer ran around the railroad tracks where he spotted a steaming locomotive and decided to use it for his getaway. As Mentzer raced to the locomotive S.H. Jackson, who was tending bar at the Little Brindle Saloon near the train station, ran out and shouted to the crowd that had gathered, "There he is." Mentzer turned, fired, and killed Jackson instantly.

The crowd rushed toward the train to catch Mentzer. Hotelkeeper Hugh Eddleson was one of the first people to reach the locomotive Mentzer had boarded for his escape. He saw a chance to grab Mentzer but Mentzer still had one bullet left in his gun and used it to kill Eddleson.

By this time, the crowd that had been attracted to the scene by the noise of gunfire became a mob of angry citizens. They boarded the locomotive and dragged Mentzer from the cab. Deputy Sheriff Dollman and fellow officer William A. Bergen, who was the deputy sheriff at the Blossburg coal camp, arrested Mentzer. They took their prisoner to the Little Brindle Saloon for safekeeping. Dollman left Bergen with their prisoner so he could telegraph Jackson's wife, who was in Topeka, to tell her that Mentzer had killed her husband.

This scene of First Street was taken around 1880. The railroad station is nearby and is the location where the chase for Mentzer occurred.

Deputy Sheriff Bergen had locked the front door to the saloon and was in the process of securing Mentzer when the mob that helped capture Mentzer started pounding on the door. The mob was led by Justice of the Peace Harvey Moulton whose partner, Eddleson had been killed earlier that evening. Moulton was angry beyond reason and demanded that Bergen turn over his prisoner for an immediate trial. Bergen refused.

Moulton kicked open the door of the saloon and rushed across the room at Mentzer. Deputy Sheriff Bergen yelled at Moulton to stop. When he didn't Bergen shot him. As Moulton was falling to the floor he shot the deputy sheriff in the stomach. Both men died during the gun battle as Mentzer escaped by running out the back door of the saloon.

By this time Moulton's mob had become a drunken posse whose only goal was to capture Mentzer and hang him. Mentzer was hiding in the alley behind the saloon when he decided he could find safety at the Williams and Fick Butcher and Bakery Shop. For some unknown reason Deputy Sheriff Dollman had a hunch that Mentzer might head for the butcher shop. Dollman arrived there just minutes behind Mentzer and arrested him. But the drunken posse also tracked Mentzer to the butcher shop.

Dollman tried to protect Mentzer but the mob overwhelmed the deputy sheriff and grabbed Mentzer. "Hang him! Hang him!" they cried out. Williams gave the mob a rope that had been used to bring a calf to the butcher shop early that morning. The mob dragged Mentzer, who was screaming, crying and pleading for his life down the street toward the Raton Bank building. There they threw the rope over the bank's sidewalk sign and hung Mentzer; who's body dangled from the bank signpost throughout the rest of the night.

This is the only known picture of Gus Mentzer's lynching in Raton.

Mentzer's body was left on display so passengers on the morning train could see the sight as a warning to other gamblers not to stop in Raton. When Mentzer's body was cut down his pockets were searched for personal belongings. All they found was a deck of cards that were distributed among the crowd as souvenirs. Two Mexican laborers were given a dollar apiece to bury Mentzer in a wooden box. However the laborers wrapped Mentzer in a blanket and threw his body in a shallow grave. They wanted the wood from the box to build a cupboard in their house.

The June 30,1882 *The Raton Guard* reported on the Coroner's Jury findings. "The Coroner's Jury acted on all cases Tuesday morning and found that Gus Mentzer came to his death by being hung by the neck by unknown parties: Harvey Moulton by a bullet fired from a pistol in the hands of Wm. A. Burgen, deputy sheriff of Blossburg; Hugh Eddleston, by a gun shot wound, the ball being fired from a pistol in the hands of Gus Mentzer; S.H. Jackson by bullets fired from a pistol or pistols in the hands of unknown parties; and William A. Burgen came to his death by a pistol shot wound received while in the execution of his duty, fired from a pistol in the hands of Harvey Moulton, Justice of the Peace."

Legal Hangings

There were only two legal hangings in Raton. David Arguello was convicted and hung for the murder of Francisco Garcia, a Colorado peace officer. The murder took place on the Floyd ranch located in Colfax County on October 19, 1905. John Medlock was convicted and hung for the murder of Carrie Boyd alias Carrie McKinney on January 4, 1901.

The Medlock sentencing took place on April 21, 1906 with Judge William J. Mills presiding. Judge Mills was Chief Justice of the Supreme Court of the Territory of New Mexico and Judge of the Fourth Judicial District Court. *The Raton Reporter* was present at the trial and reported:

"Judge Mills ordered that John Medlock, the Negro convicted of the murder of Carrie Boyd, a negress; and David Arguello, convicted of the murder of Francisco Garcia be brought into court to receive sentences." Judge Mills independently told Medlock and Arguello, "It is hereby ordered, considered, and adjudged by the court that on the 25th day of May in the year of our Lord, nineteen hundred and six, between the hours of ten o'clock in the forenoon and four o'clock in the afternoon of said day, within an enclosure to be erected by the sheriff on the court house ground in the City of Raton...be there and then hanged by the neck until you are dead...May God have mercy on your soul."

They were hung on a scaffold built in the alleyway on the West side of the County Court House, which was located at Clark Avenue and Fourth Street. Details of the actual hanging are not available because the next several issues of the *Raton Reporter* are missing from the archives.

Raton's Unsolved Murder Mystery
The Story of Prohibition Officer Ray Sutton

The War Prohibition Act, which prohibited the sale of alcoholic beverages, was passed in 1918. It became our Eighteenth Amendment, was ratified by the states, and on January 18, 1920, the United States became a legally "dry" nation.

The law was repealed by the 21st Amendment which became effective on December 5, 1933. However, during those 14 years of prohibition, the speakeasies of the roaring 20's and gangsters like Al Capone emerged. While metropolitan areas, like Chicago thrived and made headlines during the years of prohibition, illegal liquor sales and moonshine operations flourished in every town in America.

Raton was no exception. The Trinidad-Raton area was a stronghold for booze-runners. Moonshiners manufactured illegal liquor in copper stills that were scattered deep in the mountains surrounding Raton. Racketeering was big business in Colfax County.

It is not difficult to understand why moonshiners and booze-runners were abundant in the area during these years of prohibition. Many of the residents living in coal camps were immigrants who were hard working, hard drinking coal miners. They labored hard all day and when the workday was over, they enjoyed life to the fullest. Drinking was one of their cherished pastimes. Prohibition was not going to deprive them of the wine they loved to drink.

It was during these days of prohibition, the roaring 20s and 30s, that Ray Sutton, a federal prohibition officer mysteriously disappeared. Sutton was a quiet and retiring person. His many friends always found him neatly dressed and polite. Sutton's five-foot ten inch 198 pound frame was misleading and he did not appear like the tough, diligent prohibition agent that he was.

Sutton lived in Clayton, but was staying at the old Seaberg Hotel in Raton. The afternoon of August 28, 1930, he was to meet Trinidad police officer, Oscar Vandeberg. They were planning a night patrol of the Raton Pass area in search of booze runners and the slayer of Dale Kearney, a fellow officer who had been killed in Aguilar, Colorado, earlier in the month.

Sutton received a message that morning. Apparently it was important because he left his paperwork unfinished and his baggage unpacked. He jumped into his 1929 Pontiac and drove to within seven miles of Dawson where he pulled the car off the road and parked.

Colfax County Undersheriff Boots Fletcher was returning to Raton that morning when he saw Sutton sitting on the side of the road, apparently waiting to meet someone. They waved at each other, but Fletcher did not stop to talk or visit. Fletcher was the last person to see Sutton alive.

Raton History Mystery and More

More than a week passed before the *Raton Evening Gazette* carried a story headlined "Federal Prohibition Officer Ray Sutton Feared Victim of Foul Play: Last Seen August 28." Both Sutton and his Pontiac had disappeared.

A posse of over 100 men was formed and the search for Sutton began. The Colorado National Guard ordered a pilot and airplane to aid in the search. Neither the posse nor National Guard flyer found any trace of Sutton or his car.

District Attorney Fred C. Stringfellow offered a reward of $200 to anyone who discovered Sutton or his car. Within four days the reward money increased to $700 as local police officers and the Union County Commissioners added additional funds.

The State of New Mexico entered the case. New Mexico Governor Dillon made a public appeal for help and offered the State's services. Law enforcement officers from Denver to Albuquerque, as well as Federal Agents, became involved in the search for Sutton and his car. The area from Southern Colorado to Cimarron, Dawson and the Moreno Valley was searched for days.

Finally, on September 19, the *Raton Evening Gazette* ran this front-page headline: "Arrest is made in Sutton Case." James Perry Caldwell, a former Prohibition Officer who had been laid off the force because of budget cutbacks, was arrested and charged for cashing Sutton's last paycheck in the amount of $152 on September 1, four days after Sutton's disappearance..

Caldwell was charged on two counts of forging and passing a bad check. He was taken to Trinidad, where he was arraigned before U.S. Commissioner James E. Kane. Bond was set at $15,000, and when Caldwell could not meet the bond, he was sent to the Las Animas County Jail.

Later, on October 18, 1930 a cowboy, Rafael Zamora, found Sutton's car eighteen miles southwest of Koehler at the bottom of a small arroyo. It had been covered with brush and piñon trees.

"The car was found within two or three hundred yards of the open plain", *The Raton Evening Gazette* reported, " and not more than a quarter of a mile from a country highway. Ten yards from the car one could see the Taos highway with a stream of cars passing daily, yet so well was it hidden that Zamora was within a few yards of the car before he saw it."

Fingerprint experts, J.P. Clements from the state prison and J.L. Pound from Union County, were called upon to search the car for any clues that would help solve the case. Few prints of any value were found. The car had been washed and wiped clean by heavy rains.

Foul play was now a definite possibility because bloodstains were found in the back seat of the car. It is assumed that Sutton was killed outside his car and loaded into the back seat to be carried away. Because investigators thought Sutton's body could be near the car, plans were made to drag nearby Koehler

Rafael Zamora found the missing Pontiac covered with brush and pinion trees. This unpublished photograph was provided by his granddaughter.

Lake, but it was too full. The lake was eventually drained in May of 1931. Sutton's body was not found and the search proved to be completely futile.

The story of Sutton's disappearance gained national attention. Curiosity seekers arrived in droves and several fortune-tellers offered their services. One fortune-teller claimed he could find the body in less than two hours and would not charge any fee. When the officers decided to take the fortune-teller up on his offer, he failed to appear. A man, claiming to be a Federal Investigator, was arrested for being an imposter and interfering with genuine Agents working on the case.

The main suspect in the Ray Sutton case continued to be James Perry Caldwell who had forged and cashed the $152 payroll check belonging to Sutton. The check was cashed at the Santa Fe Railroad Harvey House in Trinidad. Caldwell could not raise the $15,000 bail money and was sent to the Las Animas County Jail. He was tried in federal court at Pueblo, January 15, 1931.

During the trial, Mrs. Sutton testified that the signature on the cashed check was not that of her husband. Handwriting experts backed up her testimony. They testified that Caldwell made the endorsement. Mrs. Caldwell testified her husband was home at the time and could not have cashed the check. In addition, witnesses from the Santa Fe Railroad Harvey House could not identify Caldwell as the person who cashed the check.

Caldwell had been indicted on two charges. The first was check passing and the second was forgery. The jury spent 20 hours in deliberation and on the morning of January 19, 1931 read a verdict of "Not Guilty."

Ironically, Sutton and Caldwell had been good friends for years. There was speculation that Sutton may have had unknown motives for disappearing and gave his payroll check to Caldwell to cash for him. Since there was still no trace of Sutton's body, many rumors were floating around the county. One rumor was that Sutton was still alive and working undercover in Trinidad. A pilot, Leo R. McGehee, had seen signs of smoke at irregular intervals by the edge of a plateau near Trinidad and felt the irregular pattern might be someone's signal.

There are many theories about what happened to Sutton's body. One is that he was cemented in the walls or buried under the floor of the old Raton Meat Packing Company. Another theory was that his body was dumped in a well near Colfax, which was then filled with dirt. Dawson's coke ovens are also mentioned as Sutton's burial ground as is the basement of a torn-down house in Koehler. Others theorize that he was buried under a culvert during highway construction.

The disappearance of Ray Sutton is a mystery today. Chuck Hornung wrote in the October 24, 1971 *Raton Range*, "Federal Prohibition Agent Ray Sutton is gone, but not forgotten. He lies in an unmarked grave known only to God."

Epilogue to the Ray Sutton story

I became further involved with the Ray Sutton story when Bill Darden, former Assistant District Attorney, called me one day. Darden told me that he tried to find the file on Sutton when he was working in the District Attorney's office in 1949. It was not there. The Sutton file had disappeared as mysteriously as Sutton.

John Schooley, a past president of the National Rifle Association was an investigator in the Sutton case. I called him and here are a few comments he passed on to me.

· While the search for Sutton was going on, 28 human skeletons were found. None proved to be Sutton's.

· Caldwell, the suspect who was acquitted, had a $20 gold piece in his possession with an open 'A' scratched on it. The coin was believed to have been Suttons because the open 'A' was Sutton's cattle brand.

· Sutton was reported seen alive at a racetrack in Mexico. Schooley, as part of his investigation, went to Mexico to follow up on the sighting. The trip was in vain.

The Sutton case was never closed. Years later, a young John Pobar, who shot and killed his own father for abuse, told Sheriff Barney Mitchell he saw Caldwell and Albert Sheloudy, a Cimarron bootlegger, bury Sutton's car. Mitchell, along with Schooley, went with Pobar to the area to investigate. Pobar was not able to identify the precise area and was eventually sent to Father Flannigan's Boys Town in Nebraska, where he told a priest the same story.

To this day Raton's "unsolved mystery" remains unsolved.

Murder of Raton Police Chief
Oscar Davis

The only Raton Police Chief killed in the line of duty was Oscar Davis. The murder took place on Friday, April 6, 1923. Events leading to Davis's murder began on a windy day when gust after gust of wind and dust rolled off the mountainsides into the streets of Raton.

Frances Ross, 16, was at home getting ready to attend a school dance at the gymnasium. Four of her friends, Beatrice Cleland, 13, Ollie Ferfes, 13, Dorothy Ferfes, 15, and Dorothy Wersonick, 16, were on the front porch of her house located at 220 South Second waiting for Ross to get ready for the dance. After Ross dressed she joined the girls on the porch. They decided that since they would be early for the dance, they would take a walk up the street.

They headed north towards town. Near the Fulton Market, two unidentified men in a Nash approached the girls and asked them where they were going. They replied that they were taking a walk before going to the dance. The men offered the girls a ride and the girls accepted. They drove up Third Street and turned toward Moulton. At Moulton they turned around and headed for First Street.

Raton'a Main (now Second) Street in the late 1920's.

Another car filled with teenagers going to the dance caught up with the Nash. One of the girls in the Nash said, "Don't let them pass." The driver of the Nash, who had identified himself to the girls as Clyde Norman, stepped on the gas and sped down First Street.

When they were near the Palace Hotel, Raton Police Chief Oscar Davis hailed the speeding car and ordered them to stop. Norman did not hear or see the Chief because he drove on. The girls testified later that they heard someone call, but did not know who it was.

The car drove around a second time, following the same route it had taken earlier except this time Norman went down Second Street. At the corner of Second Street and Park Avenue, Chief Davis boarded the car by jumping on the running board and ordered the men to drive to the police station. They proceeded down Park Avenue until they reached First Street, but instead of turning north towards the police station, Norman suddenly turned south.

Norman drew a concealed revolver and yelled at Davis to get off the car. Chief Davis attempted to grab the gun from Norman and at the same time with the other hand tried to cut off the switch to the car. In the struggle, Norman shot Chief Davis twice, killing him instantly.

This illustration of Chief Davis being shot is the work of Jim Mullings.

Most of the chase for the Brigance brothers took place on First Street.

Immediately after the shooting, Dorothy Wersonick jumped from the car and landed near Davis' body. Dorothy Ferfes also jumped from the car. Norman then quickly stopped the car, allowing the other girls to get out.

Officer W.T. Markham, from the coal-mining town of Swastika, chased the car down First Street. He fired his gun at the Nash until he ran out of ammunition. With his gun empty, he returned to town for reinforcements.

Meanwhile Deputy Ben Pooler heard the shooting and gave chase, but he did not shoot because he was afraid of hitting the Markham car that was chasing Norman. During the exchange of fire, one of the bullets entered the window of the Thomas building on First Street.

The speeding Nash headed North toward the railroad crossing at the end of First Street. Norman did not see the curve in the road by the tracks and rolled the car over when he could not negotiate the turn. The two men escaped uninjured and for the next 36 hours were the objects of a large-scale manhunt.

All roads were closed and guarded. Two bloodhounds from the penitentiary at Santa Fe were brought to Raton to help hunt the killers of Chief Davis. The dogs were unable to pick up the scent because the high winds continued to blanket the city with dust.

Examination of the wrecked Nash disclosed two suitcases, a sawed-off shotgun, four boxes of shells and some letters. The revolver that killed Davis was not found.

The next morning a tourist notified authorities that two men were seen on the Scenic highway about nine miles up the mountain near the Colorado border. Armed men took the bloodhounds to the scene but the dogs were unable to pick up a trail and the search was abandoned.

After they had overturned the Nash, the two men had followed the rail-road tracks for about half a mile. Then they headed for the mountains where they found a place to hide and sleep.

They remained hidden in the mountains until Saturday night, when they walked to Koehler Junction. They stopped at a ranch house where they were given a meal. After eating, they left the ranch house and followed the tracks to Maxwell.

About 6:00 P.M Sunday evening, Officer Durgeloh saw the two men near Maxwell. He talked to them for a while, but hesitated to arrest them because he was unarmed. He returned to Maxwell to get his weapons and more officers.

The officers returned to the place where Durgeloh had visited with the two fugitives and after searching for an hour and a half, found the two men hiding in a cave in the bank of the river. The men were apprehended and taken to the county jail in Raton where they were placed under heavy guard.

Sheriff Linwood interrogated both men and Assistant District Attorney Ray Stringfellow obtained statements from them confessing to the murder of Chief Davis. Both were held for trial without bond.

On Tuesday, May 8, 1923, the *Raton Reporter* featured the following story. "Clyde Norman, confessed slayer of Chief of Police Oscar Davis, has been positively identified as Newton Brigance, a brother to Oscar Brigance, who is also held in connection with the murder.

"The identification was made by O.C. Newby, Chief of Police of Cushing, Oklahoma, through photographs sent him by Sheriff Linwood. According to Chief Newby, Newton Brigance is an escaped prisoner from the jail at Stillwater where he was serving time for automobile theft. Brigance escaped from the Stillwater jail by knocking the jailer in the head."

The trial for the Brigance brothers was held in December and described by the Tuesday, December 18, 1923 edition of the *Raton Reporter* as sensational. The newspaper stated that "Perhaps no trial in the history of the county has attracted such intense and widespread interest as this, and each day's session has found the courtroom filled to capacity."

Testimony during the trial revealed that Newton Brigance, who had used the alias Clyde Norman, was born in Texas, the son of poor but respectable parents. Until he turned twenty-three, his story was one of an uneventful country boy. He was inducted into the army early in 1919 and trained as a machine gunner at Camp Travis in San Antonio, Texas. He was sent to France where he engaged in several days of battle on the St. Mihiel and Meuse-Argonne fronts, where he was gassed and shell-shocked. He was taken to a base hospital and upon his release, was sent back to the United States where he received an honorable discharge.

Newton's brother, Oscar, was also wanted by the state of Oklahoma on charges of violating his parole. He had served 26 months of a 15-year sentence for larceny of an automobile, forgery, and for assault with intent to murder.

The defense for Newton Brigance stated that, "Brigance, naturally subnormal, and of a very low grade intellect, is a bit of mental and physical wreckage since his grueling service in France." The defense further argued, "He (Newton) fired the fatal shot in what he believed to be self defense, not knowing that Mr. Davis was an officer."

Testimony given during the trial described how the Brigance brothers arrived in Raton. After Newton Brigance escaped from the state penitentiary in Oklahoma, he wandered around the countryside for several weeks. When he arrived in Ingersoll, Oklahoma, he met his brother Oscar, who was working on a farm.

Together, they set out for Prescott, Arizona, where they hoped to find work. They drove continuously from Ingersoll until they arrived in Trinidad where they stopped and had a few drinks at a local bar. Then they drove on to Raton where they picked up the five girls who were going to the school dance.

During the trial, the *Reporter* reported that Newton Brigance was loyal to his brother Oscar "to the last degree". He stoutly maintained the truth of his statements given to Linwood and Stringfellow even when hopelessly entangled in a maze of cross-examination. He contended that he did not know his brother was a fugitive from justice.

He told the court that all the firearms and ammunition in the car were his and that he himself sawed off the barrel of the shotgun found with the other effects near the wrecked car. He also said he went to a second-hand store in Raton where he traded another shotgun in his possession for the revolver that was used to kill Police Chief Davis.

The jury returned a verdict of guilty and on December 28, 1923, Newton Brigance was sentenced to hang on January 25 for the murder of Chief Davis. Oscar Brigance, who entered a plea of guilty to a charge of assault with intent to kill, was sentenced to four to five years in the state penitentiary.

The case was appealed to the State Supreme Court and a second trial was ordered. The second trial did not take place because Newton Brigance changed his plea to guilty. He was then sentenced to 95 years in the state penitentiary.

Kaniache, Chief of the Mouhache

There are many interesting stories about Indian life in Northern New Mexico and Southern Colorado. One such story involves Kaniache, chief of the Mouhaches, one of several Ute tribes located in Southern Colorado and Northern New Mexico. Kaniache was a good friend of Kit Carson and had signed a peace treaty with the whites in 1849. The treaty allowed both the Jicarillo and the Mouhache Indians to obtain food and supplies from an Indian Agency that the government had established in Cimarron, New Mexico. But the Agency often broke its promises to supply the Indians with subsistence, one problem among the many causes of turmoil among both Indians and whites.

In October 1866, Kaniache and his Utes were returning to their Colorado campgrounds from Cimarron by way of Raton Pass. They camped at one of their usual spots, the south bank of the Purgatoire River. The Indians were upset because they had been given little food and winter was about to set in. Kaniache was also angry because a drunken soldier at Cimarron had insulted him and then threatened him with a gun.

In the meantime, the Trinidad Justice of the Peace had been told that a horse was missing from a local ranch. Kaniache and his tribe were among the suspects. This suposition angered Kaniache further when the news reached his camp. To further complicate the situation, a few of the Indians had ridden their horses through some of the fields in the valley during the day. This made the settlers angry. One of the settlers rode to Fort Stevens and asked that soldiers to go after the Indians.

Kaniache thought one Ramon Vigil was the guilty party, so some of the Indians, along with Kaniache, went to confront Vigil who denied that he had stolen the horse. Vigil eventually calmed down the Indians.

After the confrontation with Vigil, some of the Indians rode through a field belonging to a Gutierrez family and started picking some unharvested corn. One of the Gutierrez boys shot at one of the Indians. The Indians jumped on their horses, ready to fight. However, by this time the soldiers from Fort Stevens arrived and a parley was arranged. Kaniache told the Lieutenant that taking the corn was not stealing because the land belonged to the Utes and that his people were hungry. After a lengthy discussion everyone settled down peaceably.

Nevertheless, the next day someone rode into town to report that the Indians were preparing to attack. The soldiers went galloping to the camp. When the Indians saw them, they jumped on their horses and galloped away. For some reason the Indians stopped, turned around and fired at the soldiers. Before dark one soldier had been killed and two wounded. Darkness stopped the battle and by daylight the Indians had vanished into the mountains.

The troop commander reported that the soldiers had killed 18 Indians, but the settlers did not believe it because they said they never saw a dead body or any signs of a dead body. However, things settled down and peace followed this incident for the time being.

Another story about Kaniache is that, after picking up food and supplies at Cimarron, the tribe would return to Walsenburg, which was at that time named The Plaza de Leones. The reason the Utes went to the Walsenburg area was because the Ute Trail was built on both sides of the village.

Kaniache liked to gamble with Fred Walsen, a trader for whom Walsenburg was named. Kaniache wanted a bright blue coat with brass buttons that Walsen wore. Walsen in return wanted some tanned buckskins like the Indians wore. It is not known if Kaniache won the coat gambling with Walsen or traded for it. One thing is certain; he got it because the following summer Kaniache was wearing the coat and a tall hat decorated with feathers.

Kaniache was not the only gambler among the Ute Indians. Many of the Indians loved to gamble. Sometimes the stakes were high and involved an offer of slavery to an opponent. Some Indian women were so addicted to gambling that they wagered household goods, clothes, and even their husband's possessions.

One of their favorite games was a game that resembled a combination of dice and poker. They used markers made from stone, bone, shells, or pieces of pottery. They were painted or marked and thrown either by hand or tumbled in baskets. Gamblers might toss six plum stones, or four in a spotted suite, or two in a stripe. Three spotted and two striped stones were like a full house in poker.

While these tales about Kaniache are interesting, it is important to realize that Indians always played an integral part in the history of New Mexico. Raton and the surrounding area were not exceptions. While there is mention of numerous tribes traveling through Colfax County, the primary tribes in Southern Colorado and Northern New Mexico were the Ute Indians. Ute Park and Ute Creek in Colfax County, for example, as well as Ute Mountain and Ute Springs in Taos Country, are names that were derived from these tribes.

At that time the Ute Indians were not well respected by many of the other tribes in New Mexico. Julian Salomon wrote in his book, *The Book of Indian Crafts and Indian Lore*, "So poorly were the tepees of the Ute constructed that they gained the tribe the name "Bad Lodges" among Indians of the plains."

For many more interesting stories about the Indians of New Mexico, visit your local library. They will be happy to locate many of the reference books available. Clara Dunning, formerly a Trinidad, Colorado, resident and historian, told me this story about Kaniache several years ago.

Raton History Mystery and More

The Indians loved to trade their handmade crafts for commercial products from merchants and citizens of the towns they passed through on their way to Cimarron. This 1882 photograph shows three Indians on a trading expedition.

Northern New Mexico Name Origins

The origin of names in Colfax County and New Mexico is fascinating because names are derived from six general language divisions. Four of the categories are Indian and the other two are Spanish and English. The four Indian languages are Tanoan, Keresan, Zuni, and Athapascan. The Tanoan language has three additional groups, namely Tiwa, Tewa, and Towa.

The languages have intermingled over the years and some very interesting names have been coined. There are also some interesting rules that govern names. For example, Indian names seldom honor an individual or place. They are almost entirely descriptive of a place.

Spanish names are also descriptive or they can focus on incidents as well as commemorate personages or places that were important to Spanish history. Albuquerque, for example, honored a Viceroy of Mexico, Don Francisco Fernandez de la Cueva Enruquez, Duque de Albuquerque.

English names follow the same pattern as Spanish names with the addition of the modern practice of merging parts of words or combining initial letters to form acronyms. For example the town of Jal, New Mexico, was named with the initials of rancher John A. Lynch. Colmor, New Mexico merged the first three letters from Colfax and Mora counties. The English language often added humorous irony, such as Humbug Creek or BellyAche Mesa.

Here are some Northeastern New Mexico names with their origins.

Towns and Places Named After Animals

Raton: The name Raton originates from the Spanish word *Ratona*, a female mouse or rat. Besides the ordinary house and field mouse, the name *Ratona* includes the rock squirrel and the kangaroo rat that flourishes in arid regions of the Western United States.

Goat Hill: Goat Hill is the bluff area where the large Raton sign can be seen from miles away, along with the star and American flag. The most common theory for the name Goat Hill is that Mexican goat herders grazed their goats on the north side of the mountain.

Cimarron: The word *cimarrón*, with an accent mark over the "o" is an Americanism in Spanish. When generalized, the word describes a wild or unruly person or untamed animal.

Crow Creek: Crow Creek flows past the ghost town of Koehler and was so named because of the vast quantity of crows that flew over the area.

Gato: Gato is derived from the Spanish word meaning cat, wildcat, or mountain lion.

Illustration by Jim Mullings

Names That Reveal Lifestyles

Tin Pan Canyon: Located a few miles West of Raton, Tin Pan Canyon was named for a shining tin pan nailed to a post by a miner as a guide and direction to his camp.

Five Dollar Canyon: Located north of Dawson, Five Dollar Canyon was named for a pioneer settler who always wanted to bet five dollars, but never had it.

Midnight: Midnight was a gold mining town in the Moreno Valley and was so named by the miners because midnight was the liveliest time of the day.

Towns and Areas Named For Geographical Peculiarities

Tenaja: Located south of Raton, *Tenaja* is Spanish for a large earthen jar for holding water or other liquids. It is close to an Indian ruin in a circular depression in the lava, which gives it the appearance of a pot or bowl.

Blind Canyon: Located at the head of the Vermejo River, cowboys called it blind because it had but one entrance.

Box Canyon: This name applies to a canyon located about three miles north of Dawson that is closed at the far end and so narrow as to make traffic through it difficult, if not impossible.

Capulin: Capulin is a Mexican-Spanish word meaning wild cherry. Capulin was first named Dedman in honor of E.J. Dedman, superintendent of the AT&SF Railroad. When Mr. Dedman died in 1914, the name was changed to Capulin because of the proximity to the volcano, Mt. Capulin.

Mt. Baldy: Located south of Raton, it was so named because of the absence of timber on its rocky summit.

Towns Named After People

Colfax: Colfax County was created on January 25, 1869 and named after Schuyler Colfax, Vice President of the United States from 1869 to 1873.

Maxwell: The village of Maxwell was named for the owner of the Maxwell Land Grant, Lucien B. Maxwell, a hunter and trapper who came to New Mexico from Kaskaskia, Illinois.

Springer: The town of Springer was the Colfax County's seat in 1882 and was named after the Springer brothers, Charles and Frank. Charles was a rancher and Frank was a lawyer and an official of the Maxwell Land Grant Company.

Folsom: Folsom is now a part of Union Country, but was once in Colfax Country and a contender for the County Seat. The town was named after President Grover Cleveland's wife, Frances Folsom.

Farley: Farley was established in 1929 and took the name of its first postmaster to serve the community.

Clayton: John C. Hill, who managed the Dorsey Ranch, founded Clayton in 1887. The town was named after Clayton C. Dorsey, the son of Senator Stephen W. Dorsey of Arkansas.

Roy: Two brothers, Frank and William Roy, established Roy in 1901. The town was named after Frank, who was the first postmaster in Roy.

Dawson: Dawson was also named after two brothers, J. B. and L. S. Dawson who were ranchers and settled on the Vermejo River in 1867.

Tolby Creek: Named after the Methodist preacher, Reverend Thomas J. Tolby, who was found murdered there. To this day the death is an unsolved mystery.

Tres Hermanos: Three peaks east of Maxwell that are close together. The name means "Three Brothers" in Spanish.

Lake Alice: Located in Sugarite Canyon, the lake was named after Alice Jeffs, the daughter of John Jeffs, who was a banker in Raton when the lake was constructed.

If you are fascinated with many of the unusual names in New Mexico, read *New Mexico Place Names, A Geographical Dictionary* edited by T.M. Pearce. It is a detailed book that contains more than 5,000 individual items that include folklore, history, and frontier humor of New Mexico.

Vermejo Park

Vermejo is derived from the Spanish word *bermejo* which means a bright reddish color. The river that flowed down the canyon was often a brick-red color and was named Vermejo by the ranchers and farmers who lived and worked along the river's bank.

Kit Carson served as a guide for explorer John Charles Fremont.

Raton History Mystery and More

Today's Vermejo Park is the heart of the Maxwell Land Grant of 1841 that encompassed nearly two million acres of land, a territory approximately the size of Rhode Island. The original land grant was called the Beaubien-Miranda Grant. To fully appreciate the complicated history of Vermejo Park, you may enjoy a basic understanding of people involved in the grant and how the it came about.

A French Canadian, Charles Hypolite Beaubien, who had studied for the priesthood in his native Quebec, moved to Taos in the 1830's where he became a prosperous Indian trader. He eventually took Mexican citizenship and changed his name to Carlos Beaubien.

On January 8, 1841, Beaubien and his friend Guadaloupe Miranda, who was the secretary of the provincial government of Santa Fe, petitioned governor Manuel Armijo for nearly two million acres of land that eventually became known as the Maxwell Land Grant. The grant was originally known and appears on all maps as the Beaubien-Miranda Grant.

Lucien B. Maxwell was a fur trapper from Kaskaskia, Illinois, who, along with Kit Carson, served as a guide to explorer John Charles Fremont on his Western expeditions. In Taos he became friends with Carlos Beaubien. On March 27, 1842 he married Beaubien's daughter, Luz, when she was only 13 years old.

Beaubien died in 1864. After his death, Maxwell and Luz began buying out the remaining heirs. By 1865 they were the sole owners of the entire Grant that included all 1,714,765 acres of pristine land.

To help develop the land, Maxwell put settlers on the range as share croppers, often giving them a small herd of cattle, sheep, or horses. The tenant agreements were always verbal and Maxwell often allowed the settlers to prosper for years without having to share in the proceeds of the land. At times Maxwell had 500 people working the land with thousands of acres under cultivation and thousands more full of sheep and cattle. Squatters were often uncontested and left alone to farm or ranch.

There were about 15 families living on the river below the ranch's headquarters. They scratched out a living from their small farms and apple orchards. Eventually they built a church, a school, and even had a bar. A Post Office was also established and managed by a Mr. Elkins.

Maxwell's fortunes, however, began to decline with the discovery of gold on the Grant in 1866. His heavy investments in gold mining ventures were a failure. Maxwell sold an option to purchase the Vermejo Ranch to three financiers for between $650,000 and $750,000. Within three months the grant was sold to an English syndicate, The Maxwell Land Grant and Railway Company for approximately $1,350,000.

Lucien Maxwell

The sale of the grant started a period of violence that was directly related to the unclear titles to the lands. The colonists resented the new absentee landlords. A Methodist minister, F.J. Tolby of Cimarron, organized a "Squatters Club" that was preparing to test the English claim in court. However, Tolby was murdered and thus began what is known as the Colfax County War.

Tolby became a martyr after his murder and another minister, Oscar P. McMains, took up the cause. For 15 years McMains was a central figure in a succession of violent conflicts between residents and company sympathizers.

In 1880 the English company sold the grant to a Dutch group that was reorganized as the Maxwell Land Grant Company. The situation worsened. The Dutch group began to evict the settlers and the squatters because they had "no papers" to prove ownership of the land. The violence did not end until the United States Supreme Court decided the ownership of the lands in 1887. The court decision confirmed ownership rights of the Dutch owners and the Colfax County War was over. This was 46 years after the original grant to Beaubien and Miranda.

Luz Maxwell

Raton History Mystery and More

At the turn of the century the Maxwell Land Grant Company began to promote the sale of their properties. In 1902 William H. Bartlett, a wealthy grain speculator from Chicago, obtained clear title to about 200,000 acres of land known as Vermejo Park and some sections of the Sangre de Cristo Grant for approximately $195,000. He later increased his holdings to well over 300,000 acres. The reason Bartlett purchased the land was because his son, William H. Bartlett, Jr., was recovering from tuberculosis and was advised to move to the Southwest.

"Old" Vermejo with the "New" house under construction on the left.

Bartlett built a cottage for his family that included room for a second son, Norman. The family moved to the ranch for the summer of 1903. Bartlett's sons lived and worked the ranch while Bartlett directed any improvements and buildings from his Chicago office by letters and telegrams. Bartlett invested substantial amounts of money in Vermejo Park.

He directed his cattle business partner, Mr. Adams, to select sites for several large lakes, an icehouse, a schoolhouse, a fish hatchery, a ranch store and numerous lodges to house guests. Eventually a power plant was built to provide electricity for the complex. Between 1907 and 1910 he built three elaborate stone residences and a greenhouse.

Bartlett moved permanently to the ranch in 1910, giving up all of his Chicago business interests. Bartlett was a generous host, sportsman, and conservationist. For example, elk were virtually non-existent at Vermejo Park. He purchased hundreds of elk, many of trophy quality, to reestablish the herd.

Bartlett died suddenly at the ranch on December 10, 1918. Ironically, his two sons died within the years following, Norman on September 1, 1919 and Will on January 5, 1920. With the death of the male Bartlett heirs, the rest of the family decided to sell Vermejo Park.

A syndicate of Chicago, St. Louis, and New York businessmen took an option to purchase the ranch. They organized The Vermejo Park Club that included family members and friends such as Tex Austin, General Billy Mitchell, Amon Carter, Douglas Fairbanks, Mary Pickford, the Frederick Guest family, the Phipps family and the David Lehmans, to name a few. Club members came to Vermejo to relax, hunt, fish, or just enjoy the beauty of the ranch. It was during this time that Mrs. Guest killed the ninth largest elk in the world. It was mounted and given to the American Museum of natural history in New York.

The Chicago, St. Louis, and New York syndicate was unable to exercise their option to purchase the ranch because they could not raise the $1,800,000 asking price and The Vermejo Park Club was eventually disbanded. From 1923 to 1926 an all-out effort was made to sell the property. Prospective buyers included the Osage Indians of Oklahoma, J.C. Penney, E.L. Doheney (of the Teapot Dome Scandal), Clarence MacKay of Postal Telegraph, Harrison Chandler of the Los Angeles Times Mirror Corporation, and several British groups.

Finally Harrison Chandler of the Los Angeles Times Mirror Corporation, along with Frank Garbutt and Bernal Dyas, purchased the ranch in 1926. They organized a new Vermejo Club that included Douglas Fairbanks, Mary Pickford, Herbert Hoover, F.W. Kellogg, Harvey Firestone, Cecil B. DeMille, Thomas W. Warner and Andrew Mellon; to name a few. Unfortunately, the depression of the 1930s took its toll and the Club was disbanded, the guest houses closed, and the land leased to rancher Ira Aten for raising cattle.

The first home where Bartlett lived. This photograph was taken in 1920.

In 1945 W.J. Gourley, a Fort Worth, Texas, native began acquiring property in the Vermejo area. He purchased 100,000 acres from the WS Land and Cattle Company ranch in Cimarron and in 1948 acquired the assets of Vermejo Park. In 1956 he purchased the Ponil Ranch from the Maxwell Land Grant Company that added an additional 96,000 acres to his holdings. Gourley continued to expand Vermejo Park until he had acquired a total of 480,000 acres, the largest single tract of the grant land.

Gourley greatly improved the wildlife on the ranch by importing elk from Wyoming, purchasing wild turkey and even started a buffalo herd. He improved all of the lakes and restored the original stone residences. A new guest operation was begun in 1952.

On December 23, 1955, the large middle guest house burned down. The loss of these facilities led to the remodeling of the stables as the main social and dining area for guests. Naturally, the new facility was named The Stables. Mrs. Gourley was also involved in the restoration process and restored Casa Grande as a residence for her own family. They moved into the home in 1963.

Mr. Gourley died in 1970 at the age of 81. After his death, the Gourley Estate sold the ranch to The Pennzoil Company. Pennzoil purchased additional land from Kaiser Coal and increased its land holding to 558,000 acres. Pennzoil operated the ranch until they sold it to Ted Turner in 1996.

Casa Grande under construction approximately 1907; before its restoration and modernization for current use.

Today the ranch is visited on a reservation-only basis. It is New Mexico's largest and best-known hunting and fishing resort, as well as a working buffalo ranch with more than 1,200 bison roaming the ranges. Elevations at the park range from 7,000 to 13,000 feet. There are 21 lakes and miles of trout streams. Six guest cottages can accommodate a maximum of 55 guests at one time.

There are over 160 species of wildlife on the park and Vermejo Park boasts the largest elk herd in New Mexico. A few species of wildlife that can be found include, for example, antelope, wild turkey, cougar, black bears, and deer. There are rainbow trout, German brown trout, Coho salmon, and the Rio Grande cutthroat trout, which is closely protected because it is nearing extinction. Most of the trout average 14-15 inches, but fishermen have reported catching trout 22 inches and weighing upwards of eight pounds.

In addition to the wildlife, there is an estimated 300-year reserve of bituminous coal, trillions of cubic feet of natural gas, and unknown quantities of oil located on the property. While coal mining operations ceased in 2002, the development of natural gas wells has had a positive impact on the economy of Raton and Colfax County. The future of Vermejo Park is indeed, very bright.

This is the main residence that Mr. Bartlett had built. In the photograph, he is standing on the balcony, on the left, wearing a white cap.

Today Casa Grande at Vermejo Park is the site's centerpiece in its lovely New Mexico mountain setting.

NRA Whittington Center

In 1973 the Raton City Commission was about to embark on a project that would be both controversial and expensive. Mayor Tony Pesavento and commissioners Charles Buttram, Gilbert Madrid, Bob Gurule and Hurley Bacon were to vote on a project to build an eight-inch pipeline to the recently acquired property line of the NRA Outdoor Center. This was to be followed by a six-inch pipeline to the Municipal Airport located at Crews Field. The cost of the project would be $750,000.

The project was controversial for several reasons. First, the citizens of Raton were concerned about Raton's water supply. Could 4,000 acre-foot Lake Maloya supply sufficient water both to the City of Raton and to the newly proposed NRA Center? Secondly, how was the cost of the proposed pipeline to be paid? Would there be water rate increases? What other taxes would increase to fund the project?

To answer these questions and fully appreciate the impact of the NRA locating in Raton, some background information is necessary.

In the early 1970's shooting ranges around the nation were decreasing. The general public then, and even today, did not want nuclear plants, waste sites, airports, or any facility that might prove dangerous, noisy or potentially unsafe near its' cities. This includes shooting ranges.

Site selection committee

NRA, realizing this, appointed a site selection committee headed by former NRA President Fred Hakenjos to secure a *fail-safe* location where urban expansion would create no problems if a shooting range was established. A *fail-safe* location is defined as one that is large enough so that any round of ammunition fired from any of the numerous shooting ranges cannot escape the property due to the property's size.

The site selection committee studied land locations in areas that stretched from Tennessee to California, from South Dakota to Wyoming, and eventually to New Mexico. Dozens of locations were given serious consideration. After months of study the Raton site was tentatively selected and a site evaluation committee was appointed. This committee's job was to put the Raton site selection under close scrutiny to be certain that the right location was selected. In addition, a consulting team of landscape architects from Kansas State University was hired to study of the Raton property for the evaluation committee.

When the State of New Mexico learned it was in the running for the shooting range, then Governor Bruce King appointed Ladd Gordon, Director of the New Mexico Game and Fish Department to assist the NRA with its site selection. In addition, Raton citizens Richard Segotta, Alvin Stockton, Jim Roper and Mayor Tony Pesavento formed a committee that would help obtain information and statistics on the Raton site. For the NRA, perhaps the most instrumental person involved in the site selection process was George Whittington, an attorney from Amarillo, Texas. Whittington was a highly regarded NRA board member. He loved the mountain states and was a frequent visitor to the Raton area. He was an active oilman and had spent a lifetime buying, selling, trading, and swapping land and mineral rights.

With the help of people like George Whittington and the involvement of state and local officials, Raton was selected as the best possible site for NRA's shooting range. The next step was to convince the entire NRA Board of Directors that Raton was the right choice.

NRA Board visits Raton site

In August of 1973, 60 NRA Board members flew to Raton to investigate the site. The area at that time was mostly inaccessible by automobile and many Raton citizens donated their time and four-wheel drive vehicles to give the NRA board members a first hand look at the site selected.

After their tour of the Raton site, the NRA Board returned to Denver, where a special directors' meeting was being held. A roll call vote was taken. The vote was 56 in favor of acquiring the Raton site with six members voting no. The first big hurdle had been cleared, but little did anyone realize the near catastrophes that were about to occur.

The city commission proceeded with plans to construct the pipeline that would furnish water to the NRA property and to Crews Field. However, controversy among the citizens of Raton continued regarding the supply of water and the cost of the pipeline.

The city commission, however, was determined to meet its commitment and authorized a bond issue in the amount of $750,000. The bonds were funded through FmHA on July 1, 1976 with a five- percent interest rate. They were to be paid over a 40-year period with the final payment due in 2016.

Before the pipeline could be built, titles to the NRA site had to be cleared. Obtaining the land necessitated a complex series of land swaps. Ironically, not a single square foot of land on the NRA Center was purchased. It was all traded, thanks to the skills of George Whittington and the property owners who were willing to sacrifice portions of their land to make the NRA Center a reality.

Alvin Stockton traded land he owned for land near Kiowa and the TO Ranch. Annita Van Bruggen sold portions of her land to NRA who in turn traded land to Annie Ruth Bell. Kaiser Steel traded part of its' Raton land for industrial property purchased by NRA in California. Finally NRA had a center. The pipeline was eventually completed and some minor construction began at the site. But everything was not peaches and cream.

The first sign locating the site of the incoming NRA facility.

NRA membership uproar

In 1977 at the NRA annual meeting in Cincinnati, an internal rift occurred within the NRA membership. Some members did not want NRA dues monies to be used to finance the Center's projects. General Maxwell Rich, who was then executive vice-president of NRA and instrumental in locating the Center in Raton, was fired.

The end result of the Cincinnati meeting was passage of an NRA by-law that stated that dues monies from the general membership would not used for the Raton center. Subsequently, the NRA Special Contribution Fund was formed to finance and develop the center. From 1979 to 1983 barely enough money was raised for the center to exist and build a few projects. But the fund raising program worked. Today the Center is financially stable and is completely self-sufficient.

Whittington Center Trivia

When Harold Butt, a local contractor, was asked to drive a bulldozer to clear the proposed property boundary between Kaiser and the NRA Center, George Whittington walked in front of the bulldozer and placed colored engineer tape on the property line. This type of dedication by Whittington is the reason the Center was eventually named in his honor.

NRA Whittington Center (pictured) was the second name change for the Center. First it was known as the NRA Outdoor Center. Later the name was changed to NRA Whittington Center.

An impressive sign and landscaped small park locate the entrance to the NRA Whittington Center.

To assure independence of the Center, The Special Contribution Fund Board of Trustees was appointed to oversee the activities and set a budget. Frank Foote was the original director of the Center until August 1986, when the Center's Board decided to reorganize management. Mike Ballew, a proven land management expert, was then hired as the Centers' director and Frank Foote became Fiscal Manager and handled the fund raising activities.

Whittington Center's phenomenal growth

The growth of The Whittington Center has been phenomenal since its beginning in 1973. In 1986 there were 7,460 visitors to the Center. Today, visitations to the center exceed the 100,000 mark.

Approximately $11 million has been spent on improvements to the 33,300-acre property. Here is a listing of just a few of those improvements.

- In 1982 an office and maintenance shop were built.
- The Ajax Class Room building was erected in 1985 and seats 75 people. More than 2000 student days are spent in the Ajax building annually.
- A housing complex, with modified dorm-style rooms that would accommodate 90 people, was built in 1988.
- Construction of a Log Cabin Complex, to sleep 135, begam soon after.
- During the same year, a 250 seat dining facility was completed.
- 125 hookups were installed for recreational vehicles.
- The shotgun complex was improved and features 11 trap ranges, four skeet ranges and two five-stand ranges. Additionally, a 28-station sporting clay range has been built.
- In 1990 The Whittington Welcome Center was built at a cost of $500,000.
- The Center built the largest complement of silhouette ranges in the nation.
- The largest bench rest range in the nation was built at the Center.
- 100 Firing point high power rifle ranges with firing lines from 200 to 1,000 yards have been constructed.
- There are action pistol/Old West shooting ranges.
- A variety of law enforcement ranges are available at the center.

The NRA Whittington Center is the most comprehensive shooting range in the nation where more than 200 scheduled events are held annually. They include competitive, educational, recreational, and research oriented activities.

Funded entirely by voluntary contributions, NRA Whittington is truly a unique facility that attracts visitors to the Raton area who are encouraged to visit the Center where more information can be obtained. A short video is available at the Center headquarters that highlights many of the Center's points of interest and activities.

Many matches are held throughout the year. This contestant is preparing for the National 50-Caliber contest on the 1000-yard range.

Diversification is a keynote to all NRA Center activities, such as this Archery Hunter Education Challenge underway on the Coors range.

The NRA Whittington Center Welcome Center and Administration Building located only a few minutes from Raton.

The Story of Jim Pappas

Several of my friends who knew I was writing this book told me that I should include the story of my dad. The reason, they told me, is because in one sense he was typical of the many immigrants who settled in this country. Yet, in another sense, he was not typical because he was an entrepreneurial person, a characteristic not found in most immigrants.

Jim Pappas, born Demitri Papadomanolakis, on the island of Crete on June 21, 1893 left his homeland at the age of 17 in quest of a new life in America, the Land of Golden Opportunity. He recalled the tears that flowed from his eyes as his ship approached the Statue of Liberty. When they docked in New York Harbor, all he possesed was a $20 dollar gold piece, the desire for freedom and high hopes of becoming a part of this country. He spoke no English.

He settled in New York for a few months and then moved to Detroit where he worked as a laborer with the Ford Motor Company. A fellow country-man wrote and told Pappas of the good life and money to be made in the coal camps of Northern New Mexico. He was intrigued with the possibilities and before long found himself working in coal mines in and around Colfax County. He worked underground mining coal for about $2.00 a day and saved every penny he could. For the next six years his only dream was to earn enough money to start a business of his own.

He clearly remembered the day he quit mining. He was pushing a loaded coal car when it jumped the track. He unloaded the coal, replaced the car on the track, reloaded the coal and started to push again. Once again the car jumped the track. With deep despair he threw his tools into the car, walked out of the mine, threw a chunk of coal back over his shoulder and headed to Raton.

With money saved, he purchased 544 goats from a rancher in Mora, New Mexico. With the aid of a helper they walked the goats 150 miles to what is now the TO Ranch near Raton and started a goat cheese business.

As the story goes, goat cheese was not the only product Pappas manu-factured. These were the years of Prohibition and Greeks knew how to make excellent wine and moonshine. Pappas was earning and saving the money he needed to start the business in town that he had always dreamed of having. However, his business career quickly ended when he was drafted into the United States Army where he served until the end of World War I.

In 1922, he purchased the Busy Bee Hotel with the profits he made from the goat cheese (and moonshine) business. Within a year he sold the hotel and moved to Denver looking for another business to invest in. A friend interested him in the candy making business and he returned to Raton to establish a candy and ice cream shop.

Dimitri Papadomanolakis (Jim Pappas) in one of his favorite photographs. This was taken in his Sweet Shop, when it was located in downtown Raton, sometime during the 1940s.

This is the original candy shop purchased by Pappas and Petritsis. The small building on the left was the McAntosh Restaurant. Pappas & Petritsis eventually purchased that restaurant building and increased the size of their shop to include a complete soda fountain.

In 1923, he and his partner, Gus Petritsis, opened the Corner Candy Kitchen. They operated the shop for 36 days before selling it to Eric Kintsel and Marcum Honeyfield. The reason they decided to sell the shop was because Pappas and Petritsis wanted a larger building that would house a soda fountain with table seating. The same year they purchased the original Sweet Shop from Tom Logan and on November 9th opened for business.

This 1925 photograph shows the inside of the Sweet Shop after it was combined with the McAntosh restaurant building. Note the candy cases to the left which displayed more than 120 varieties of candy.

Raton History Mystery and More

Pappas had never married. It was 1933 and he was approaching 40 years of age when an uncle (who was a Greek priest) in Greece wrote and told him about a lovely young lady of marriageable age. He returned to Greece, met and courted Katherine Tornazakis. She was 19. Within a few months they were married. They returned to Raton where he continued in the candy and ice cream business with his partner, Gust Petritsis. When Petritsis retired in the early 1950s, Pappas purchased the remaining interest in the Sweet Shop and, with Katherine's help, ran the Sweet Shop for many more years. Jim Pappas passed away on November 12, 1971. Katherine joined him on April 4, 1987.

My dad never talked much about his moonshine days, but many old timers told me stories of some of his activities. For example, I always wondered why he purchased the goats in Mora, which is just a few miles northwest from Las Vegas, New Mexico. The story goes that the goats were not only herded to the TO Ranch, but often as far as Nebraska. I also wondered why they purchased goats and not sheep or cattle. The reason was because the Greeks knew how to herd goats. Goats were, (and still are) a popular farm animal in Greece while sheep and cattle are not.

The reason the goats were herded over such a large territory, I was told, is because of the cliental for the moonshine. It appears that there were numerous red light districts along the way that needed quality liquor for their customers. In addition, there were also numerous ranches and farms that had to be supplied. I suppose those were the days when a merchant took his wares to the customer rather than a customer going to the merchant. Besides, many of the farms along the way were also the primary suppliers of the ingredients that went into the moonshine.

Since making moonshine was illegal, the mountains and hidden valleys along the way were excellent places to stop and not only rest for a few days, but an opportunity to make a few more gallons of moonshine for the next series of customers down the road.

A memorable story tells of when my dad ran a café on First Street. The name of the café has been lost in history. Apparently, it was a front for selling moonshine to local Raton residents and miners in the area. The café was located in a two-story building with moonshine stored on the second floor. A "water line" was installed which lead to the café located on the first floor. It was labeled "Cold water." Whenever a customer came in and wanted his jug filled with spirits, café employees simply turned on the cold-water spigot and filled the customer's jug.

Ben Zeller, a friend of mine, purchased that building in the 1990s. He told me that he found several pipelines on the second floor that lead to nowhere on the first floor. In addition, he discovered a hidden trap door that lead to the basement, where a cache of old bottles filled with wine was buried in the ground.

The wine had turned to vinegar, but the evidence was strong that the building had once been used as an outlet for homemade wine and moonshine.

There is an interesting epilogue to these and many of the other wonderful stories I have heard over the years about the immigrants who came to this country. These people were not criminals. They were honest, hard-working, people who wanted to succeed in this country. It is obvious that, not only my dad, but many of the other successful business people, could not start a business making a two dollars a day in the coal mines. They had to engage in activities that were basically illegal in those days, which included making moonshine and operating red-light districts. But, when the days of prohibition were over, these people became civic and business leaders of their communities. This is not only true in Raton, but in hundreds of communities throughout this country.

One reason why people like my dad never talked much about these activities is because they knew they were engaged in an illegal activity. While it provided the means to gain the financing they needed to get into a legitimate business, they were not necessarily proud of the fact that they were breaking the law. What mattered to them, their families, and friends was that they were successful in their lives and contributed to society.

There were no shopping malls in the 1940s and teenagers did not have cars to "drag Main Street." Their hangouts were places like the Sweet Shop (with its new facade), Sally's Sugar Bowl, Jone's Drug Store, Arnold's Drug Store, Vandenburg's Malt Shop or Wright's Steaks and Shakes...to name a few of Raton's youth hangouts.

Raton History Mystery and More

Photo   Gallery

While researching this book, I came across hundreds of photographs that were absolutely wonderful. Many, however, were so old and faded that they were difficult to copy. Nor could we use them all in this book because of space limitations. At the last minute, my publisher and I decided we should add a few more, so here are samples of the best.

Page 102: This is the Willow Springs Ranch around 1880. The ranch was the first stop and resting place for travelers after crossing the mountains from Trinidad on the Santa Fe Trail. Several years ago there were many Raton citizens who started a campaign to change Raton's name back to Willow Springs. They thought it was more romantic than Raton.

Page 103: My favorite old photo, of someone looking down onto Raton from Goat Hill, is this 1882 picture. When I see it I think to myself, "What a great place to go, and sit, and think about affairs of the world." Sometimes solitude is wonderful.

Page 104: Every time I see this photo I wonder what possessed so many people to climb Raton Mountain just to have their picture made. In the lower left side of this print you will see a goat. Old timers tell us that the name of Raton Mountain was changed to Goat Hill because so many goat herders grazed their flocks in the mountainous area.

Page 105: I could probably write another book on only the sports activities in Colfax County. It seems like the two most popular pastimes for coal miners were drinking and sports. This is the Blossburg baseball team in 1889.

Page 106: There are many people who do not believe that Raton ever saw oil drilling. This is a 1902 photo of Raton's first oil well.

Page 107 I mentioned the great apple orchards of Colfax County earlier in this book. This 1915 photograph is of the apple orchard on the Urraca Ranch outside Cimarron.

Page 108: I'm partial to this photograph of Second Street taken in 1922. My reason is that if you look at the right-hand side of the picture you will see part of the old Sweet Shop sign above the lone person walking down the street.

Page 109: The coal miners of Colfax County were proud of their heritage, their work and their community. I would wager that not a single miner was absent when this picture of the Koehler miners was taken in 1951.

Page 110: There are two sets of these red brick charcoal ovens located about 30 miles northwest of Raton along the Canadian River, and about one mile east of what was once the town of Catskill. Here, logs were converted to charcoal that shipped to smelters. The land is now owned by Vermejo Park. The story of Catskill is very interesting and, fortunately, both the Arthur Johnson Memorial Library and Raton Museum have considerable files of history and number of photographs about Catskill.

Page 111: This photograph gives you an idea of the size of the charcoal ovens. The protected area is now closed to the public.

Willow Springs Ranch in the 1880 period of its existence.

Raton from Goat Hill in 1882

Raton   History   Mystery   and   More

On Goat Hill, with a grazing goat in the lower left.

Blossburg Baseball Team 1889

Raton History Mystery and More

In 1902 this first oil well was drilling in Raton

Raton History Mystery and More

Apple Orchard on the Urraca Ranch near Cimarron

Raton's Second Street in 1922, Sweet Shop sign on the right.

Koehler Coal Miners, 1951

Raton History Mystery and More

Red brick charcoal ovens near the Canadian River.

Size of the ovens dwarfs the visitor's vehicle.

Thank you, Thank you, Thank you!

It takes the help of many people and numerous resources to write a book about historical events. Without them this book would have been impossible to assemble. I am forever grateful for their contributions.

- **Leslie Pappas.** Leslie is my niece and a reporter for the *Philadelphia Inquirer*. When I asked her to edit this book, I told her to be a "tough" editor. She was! Her editing and suggestions took this book from grade-school level to a professional level.
- **Roger Sanchez.** Roger is the curator at the Raton Museum. Most of the photographs in this book are from the museum's collection. Roger spent hours gathering pictures that were appropriate for many of the stories in this book.
- **Jim Mullings.** Jim is a retired school teacher and very talented artist. All of the artwork in this book is a result of Jim's artistic talent and imagination. Since there were no photographs available for several stories, Jim created an artist's conception of what probably happened.
- **Tom Burch.** Tom is a former curator of the Raton Museum and one of the most knowledgeable people of Raton history that I know. Several of the photographs in this book came from Tom's personal collection of Raton memorabilia.
- **Ann C. Haslanger.** Ann's "A History of Vermejo Park", written in 1982, was one of my main resources on the history of Vermejo Park. Her eight-page booklet was well researched and probably as accurate as any story written about Vermejo Park.
- **Clara Dunning.** Clara was a resident and avid historian of Trinidad, Colorado. She loved the history of the Indians in Southern Colorado and told me the story of Kaniache years ago. She allowed me to use as much of her research as I needed when I began writing the Vermejo story.
- **Denise Gallegos.** Denise was working for the State of New Mexico, Energy, Minerals, and Natural Resources Department when we met. She was instrumental in sending me the New Mexico State Inspector's report on the Dawson Mine explosion of 1913 and well as the list of miner's who died in that mine disaster.
- **Evlyn Shuler.** Evlyn lived just a block away from my house and we often visited about Raton history. She had given me a "white paper" she had written about Raton and her father, Dr. Shuler, that I used as reference material for this book.

Raton History Mystery and More

- **Kenneth Fordyce.** Mr. Fordyce wrote a story about Willow Springs that is a wonderful reference. His story is available at the Raton Library for anyone who would like to learn more about the Willow Springs Ranch and its many visiting travelers.
- **Ricardo Garcia.** Ricardo is a former resident of Raton and the coal camps. He is a professor at the University of Nebraska and writes a column for the *Raton Range* called "Coal Camp Days". Some of his information was used in this book.
- **Chuck Hornung.** Chuck wrote "The Lynching of Gus Mentzer" that was the basis for most of my story on "The Most Violent Day in Raton's History." He also wrote a series of articles for our *Raton Range* on the disappearance of Ray Sutton. Both of his stories were invaluable in my research and writings.
- **Mike Ballew.** Mike is the current Director of NRA Whittington Center. Mike helped me authenticate the history of the Center.
- **Steven A. Giordano.** Steven is Assistant Program Director at the NRA Whittington Center. He located several of the photographs used in the NRA story.
- **Bill Donati.** Bill is a life long resident of Raton and very active with the Shuler Theatre. Bill supplied me with historical information on the Shuler Theater.
- **Bill Fegan.** Bill was instrumental in developing theater in Raton. He has directed many excellent shows at the Shuler and brought many nationally known shows to Raton.
- **Susie Turner.** Susie lives in Albuquerque, NM but has a keen interest in Raton. Susie helped with final editing of this book.
- **Melody Mascarenas.** Melody is a resident of Raton and also helped with the final editing.
- **Sherman and Elizabeth Bennett.** Besides contributing several photographs used in the Vermejo Park story, Mrs. Bennett told me several stories about the building of the mansion at Vermejo.
- **Joe and Barbara Aldaz:** The Aldaz'es were gracious enough to bring me several old postcards to use in the book.
- **Joe and Wilma Malovich:** Joe and Wilma have a large collection of old photographs that I was hoping to use, especially of the charcoal ovens at Vermejo which are in the photo gallery.
- **John and Catherine Gabriele.** When I first wrote the story about Ray Sutton, John and I walked several miles at various locations trying to find where Sutton might be buried. Naturally, we did not find his grave. Catherine also let me use several old photographs she had in her files.

- **Frank Mahannah and Pat French.** Frank and Pat were gracious to me in finding photographs of The City of Bethlehem.
- **The ladies at the Colfax County Clerks office.** All of the old newspapers dating back to the late 1880's are archived at the County Clerk's Office. They are bound by years, and some collections are very heavy and bulky. The ladies not only helped me find the years I was researching, but helped me lift the volumes from the shelves.
- **The Staff at The Authur Johnson Memorial Library.** The entire staff at the Library went out of their way to help me find photographs and articles from newspaper clippings.
- **Bill Carroll,** a new resident of Raton and a very welcome one. He hails from San Diego and is a book publisher. Bill took my manuscript to polish and publish it. Without Bill, this book would still be a draft in my computer.

- **And,** for those many others whose kind words encouraged me:
Thank you again and again.
M.J.P.

Printed in the United States
30544LVS00001B/370-459